The Icelandic Saga

PETER HALLBERG

The Icelandic Saga

Translated with Introduction and Notes

by Paul Schach

UNIVERSITY OF NEBRASKA PRESS · LINCOLN · 1962

First Bison Book printing March, 1962
Most recent printing shown by first digit below:

7   8   9   10

Swedish edition published by Svenska Bokförlaget under the
title *Den isländska sagan.*

Preface

PETER HALLBERG'S *Den isländska sagan* is the most readable
and reliable introduction to the Sagas of Icelanders to come
to my attention since the publication of Sigurður Nordal's
remarkable monograph *Sagalitteraturen* (1953). Indeed,
these two slender volumes supplement each other in a most
fortunate manner. Whereas Nordal's treatise presents a concise, lucid delineation of the development of Old Icelandic
prose writing in general (with major emphasis, of course, on
the classical sagas), Hallberg's study comprises a perceptive
analysis of salient features of the substance and form of the
Icelandic sagas of native heroes together with a penetrating,
sensitive interpretation of several masterpieces of this literary genre. Although Hallberg may differ somewhat in
detail or emphasis with Nordal and Einar Ólafur Sveinsson,
he is in essential agreement with these eminent leaders of
the realistic "Icelandic school" of saga research, whose revo-
lutionary findings he discusses and utilizes with critical
acumen. This fact alone warrants the translation of his book
on the sagas, for the Icelanders' views of the origin, composition, and significance of their ancient prose literature
have still not found proper recognition among educated
laymen or even among scholars not conversant with Modern
Icelandic.

In general I have tried to make my translation as faithful as the individuality of the author's style and the seman-
tic and idiomatic differences between Swedish and English
permit. I have not hesitated, however, to translate rather
freely in spots or to make such modifications in the text and
critical apparatus as I deemed desirable for English as opposed to Scandinavian readers. Several changes, including a

few minor omissions, were suggested by the author himself. Occasionally my interpretations of the Icelandic quotations will be found to differ slightly from those of Mr. Hallberg. The purpose of the introductory essay and the additional annotation is to furnish pertinent background information and to facilitate the enjoyment and further study of the sagas as well as other forms of Old Icelandic literature which one should know in order to appreciate the sagas fully. I have incorporated into the Introduction as many as possible of the author's references to literature on the sagas, omitting only the titles of several Swedish translations, for which I have substituted English or German ones. Additional notes and additions to the author's notes are indicated by an asterisk (*).

In the treatment of personal and place names I have followed the practice of the author in rather consistently retaining the Icelandic forms. The pronunciation of these names should not cause any great difficulty for the reader. The consonants þ and ð correspond to the voiceless and voiced continuant *th* in *thin* and *then,* respectively. The vowels ö and ø correspond to German ö, *y* is sounded like German ü, and the digraph *æ* is pronounced like German ä. The remaining vowels and consonants as well as the diphthongs have approximately the same values as in German except that *ei* and *ey* rime with English *day*. Vowel length is indicated by an acute accent. Stress is on the first syllable.

As a designation for the classical sagas I have avoided the conventional term "Family Sagas," both because the Icelanders themselves deplore it as misleading and because it is reminiscent of outdated romantic postulates regarding the genesis and nature of this literary genre. Instead, I have used "Sagas of Icelanders," which literally translates the Icelandic word *Íslendingasögur,* or "Icelandic sagas of native heroes," which describes these epic narratives and differentiates them from the various other kinds of prose works known as sagas.

Persons unfamiliar with the Icelandic sagas of native heroes might do well to read the analysis of several major sagas (Chap. 10) before plunging into the somewhat complex controversy about the origin and transmission of the literary genre (Chap. 5) and the penetrating discussions of salient features of the form and substance of the sagas (Chaps. 6–9, incl.).

It is a pleasant duty to acknowledge the help of my wife, Ruth Yohn Schach, in the editing and translation of this volume. She not only typed the manuscript, read proof, and prepared the index; she also eliminated numerous Germanisms and Swedicisms from my translation and in general improved the style.

Contents

Translator's Introduction

THE POETRY AND PROSE of medieval Iceland constitute the most unique and probably the richest and most varied literature of any country of Europe in the Middle Ages. Although its intrinsic artistic merit has not always been fully appreciated, this literature has long been esteemed by antiquarians in England, Germany, and Scandinavia, both as a source of "history" and as a sort of substitute for their own lost poetry of pre-Christian times. Except for a few lays preserved in Old English and Old High German, the pagan heroic verse once common to all Germanic peoples has survived only in Icelandic manuscripts. Similarly the mythological poetry which flourished in the North before the introduction of Christianity has come down to us only in Icelandic form. Thus the *Poetic Edda*, as the chief collection of these lays is known, is a treasure house of inestimable value for students of Germanic heroic legend and Norse mythology. Together with Snorri Sturluson's *Prose Edda* and the considerable corpus of skaldic verse (see Chap. 4), these poems are our main source of information on the deities of ancient Scandinavia and the poetic and legendary heroes of Germania.

Like the Eddic poems, the verses of the skalds—as the professional poets of Norway and Iceland were known—have been preserved for posterity almost exclusively by the Icelanders. Skaldic poetry shares the alliteration and strophic form of the Eddic lays. Otherwise, however, it differs radically from all other kinds of Germanic verse. Many of these poems were declaimed by their authors before the princes in whose honor they were composed. Skaldic verse is syllabic, and its most characteristic meter, the *dróttkvætt*, employs internal rime and consonance. The skalds were fond of kennings, involved metaphors based largely on pagan mythology. It is largely due to the sheer complexity of its structure that so much skaldic poetry has been preserved. Although it originated in Norway, the skaldic art soon became an Icelandic monopoly, and the leading court poets in Norway for over two centuries were Icelanders. The importance of this verse for the Sagas of Icelanders and the Sagas of Kings is very great.

While the chief merit of the Icelanders in the areas of Eddic and skaldic poetry was the preservation and cultivation of traditional forms, they were true innovators in the field of prose composition. During the twelfth and thirteenth centuries, when there was practically no writing of vernacular prose in Europe, Icelandic authors created a narrative prose which, at its best, is characterized by a psychological realism and by a sophistication and subtlety of style which are the despair of modern translators. Sigurður Nordal divided these narratives into sagas of ancient, former, and contemporary times. The Sagas of Icelanders, with which Hallberg is primarily concerned, belong to the second of these groups. The main representative of the third group is *Sturlunga saga*, which Hallberg also discusses in some detail. Consequently I shall limit my comments on Old Icelandic prose to the first group of sagas, which are treated only briefly by the author in his chapter on the decline of saga writing, and which, in general, have received only scant attention in the standard handbooks and histories of Old Icelandic literature.

The sagas of ancient times fall into two subgroups: the *fornaldarsögur* proper, or mythical-heroic sagas, and the *riddarasögur* ("Sagas of Knights"), or romances of chivalry. These correspond in origin and content to the Middle High German *Heldenepos* ("Heroic Epic") and *Ritterepos* ("Courtly Epic"). The former derive from lays and legends of Germanic heroes from the time of the Great Migrations or from Viking times. To this group belong such works as *Völsunga saga* ("The Saga of the Volsungs"), a prose paraphrase of the Eddic poems of the Nibelungen cycle and the chief source of Wagner's *Ring*; *Þiðriks saga,* a voluminous conglomeration of tales loosely grouped about the famous Dietrich of Bern; *Hrólfs saga kraka,* which relates to early Danish and Swedish history; *Heiðreks saga,* which preserves some of the oldest Germanic verse; and *Örvar-Odds saga,* ably discussed by the author (Chap. 11). The *riddarasögur* are, as the name suggests, prose adaptations of foreign romances. These include *Tristrams saga,* the only complete member of the Thomas group of Tristan romances (to which Gottfried's Middle High German *Tristan und Isolde* also belongs); *Karlamagnús saga,* a lengthy saga of Charlemagne based on French and Latin sources; and translations of the *lais* of Marie of France and of several Arthurian romances of Chrestien de Troyes. Although the artistic merit of the sagas of ancient times is far inferior to that of the Sagas of Icelanders or the Sagas of Kings, they are of considerable importance to the literary historian. The first group has preserved Germanic lays and legends that would otherwise have been forgotten, while some of the translations and adaptations of foreign romances are important for the reconstruction of lost or poorly preserved originals. Furthermore these works are one of the chief sources of the so-called *lygisögur* and the *rímur,* which helped preserve the continuity of the Icelandic language and Icelandic literature. It may be of interest to future scholars in Germanic philology to know that this neglected field of study offers great possibilities for research.

The number of English translations of Old Icelandic verse and prose works is slowly but steadily growing. The anthology *A Pageant of Old Scandinavia* (1946), edited by Henry Goddard Leach, shows the amazing scope and variety of the ancient and medieval literatures of the North. The

most extensive collection of translations of Old Icelandic
and Old Norwegian literature is the twenty-four-volume
Sammlung Thule, edited by Felix Niedner. (Unless otherwise indicated, all German translations referred to hereafter
belong to this collection.) Excellent translations of the
Poetic Edda have been made by Henry Adams Bellows
(1926) and by Lee M. Hollander (1928, new rev. ed.,
1962). The German translation of Felix Genzmer, which
has undergone several editions, has won high praise from
Icelanders. Hollander's *Old Norse Poems* (1936) contains
the most important non-skaldic verse not included in the
Poetic Edda proper, and his book *The Skalds* (1946) is the
best study and anthology of skaldic verse in English. The
Prose Edda in somewhat abridged form is available in a
German translation by Gustav Neckel and Felix Niedner
(1925). The English translations by A. G. Brodeur (1916)
and by Jean I. Young (1954) are also abridged, treating
primarily the *Gylfaginning* (see Chap. 4).

Since most of the sagas of ancient times and their late
adaptations and derivatives (*lygisögur*) appeal to a smaller
audience than the Sagas of Icelanders and the Sagas of
Kings, relatively few of them have been translated into
English. *Survivals in Old Norwegian of Mediaeval English,
French, and German Literature* (1941) by H. M. Smyser and
F. P. Magoun contains excerpts from *Karlamagnús saga*
and *Þiðriks saga* and selections from the *Strengleikar* ("Breton Lays"). *Þiðriks saga* is available in a German translation
by Fine Erichsen (1924). *The Saga of the Volsungs* (1930)
by Margaret Schlauch includes a translation of *Ragnars saga
loðbróks*. *Heiðreks saga* was recently edited by Christopher
Tolkien with an English translation (1960). A translation
of *Hrólfs saga kraka* is included in Gwyn Jones' *Eirik the
Red and Other Icelandic Sagas* (1961). Roger Sherman
Loomis' reconstruction of *The Romance of Tristram and
Ysolt by Thomas of Britain* (new rev. ed., 1951) is based
largely on *Tristrams saga ok Isöndar*. My translation of this

saga will be published shortly by the University of Nebraska Press. *Sturlunga saga* is available in a complete Danish translation by Kr. Kålund (1904) and in an abridged German version by W. Baetke (1930). One of the sagas comprising this compilation, the *Saga of Hrafn Sveinbjarnarson*, was translated into English by Anne Tjomsland (1951). Two of the Sagas of Bishops are available in English translation: *The Life of Lawrence* (*Laurentius saga*) by Oliver Elton (1890) and *The Life of Gudmund the Good* by G. Turville-Petre and E. S. Olszewska (1942).

Modern translations of most of the major Sagas of Icelanders have been made recently. *Njáls saga* can be read in an American translation of Bayerschmidt and Hollander (1955) and in a British one by Magnús Magnússon and Hermann Pálsson (1960). *Egils saga* was translated by Gwyn Jones (1960). A translation of *Laxdæla saga* by Margaret Arent is forthcoming. A translation of *Eyrbyggja saga* by P. Schach (Introduction and verse translations by Lee M. Hollander) was published in 1959. *Grettis saga* is available in an older translation by Samuel Laing (1914). Among the recent collections of translations of shorter sagas are *Four Icelandic Sagas* (1935) and *Eirik the Red and Other Icelandic Sagas* (1961), both by Gwyn Jones. The former contains *Hrafnkels saga*, *Þorsteins saga hvíta*, *Vápnfirðinga saga*, and *Kjalnesinga saga*; the latter includes, in addition to the mythical-heroic saga mentioned above, five Sagas of Icelanders and three *þættir*: *Hænsna-Þóris saga*, *Vápnfirðinga saga*, *Þorsteins þáttr stangarhöggs*, *Hrafnkels saga*, *Eiríks saga rauða* (from which the collection receives its title), *Þiðranda þáttr*, *Auðunar þáttr vestfirzka*, and *Gunnlaugs saga*, which has been translated more often than any other saga. Gwyn Jones has also done a translation of *Vatnsdæla saga* (1944). *Three Icelandic Sagas*, translated by M. H. Scargill and Margaret Schlauch (1950), contains *Gunnlaugs saga*, *Bandamanna saga*, and *Droplaugarsona saga.* Translations of *Kormáks saga* and *Fóstbrœðra saga* by Lee M. Hollander appeared under the title *The Sagas of Kormák and the Sworn Brothers* (1949). Of especial interest to American readers is Einar Haugen's *Voyages to Vinland* (1942), in which the translator has harmonized the two versions of the story and supplemented them from other sources. The translation is accompanied by an excellent commentary and adequate notes.

Snorri's *Heimskringla* is available in translations by Samuel Laing (1894) and by E. Monsen and A. H. Smith (1932). The latter was not made from the original, however, but from a Norwegian translation. The translation of *Orkneyinga saga* by A. R. Taylor (1938) is especially important for its excellent introduction, which is based largely on Nordal's edition of that saga. The only faithful English translation of *Jómsvíkinga saga* is that of Lee M. Hollander (1955).

As already indicated, most of the sagas and *þættir* mentioned here as well as many others are included in the *Sammlung Thule.* Excellent Danish, Norwegian, and Swedish translations of the Sagas of Icelanders and the Sagas of Kings have also been published during the past several decades.

In recent years several important editions of the Sagas of Icelanders have appeared. For students, the eighteen-volume *Altnordische Sagabibliothek* (1892–1929) is almost indispensable. Although outmoded in some respects the critical apparatus is very helpful. *Íslenzk fornrit* (1933–) includes the definitive editions of the Sagas of Icelanders and of Snorri's *Heimskringla.* The lengthy introductions are extremely valuable, but can be used only by those who read Modern Icelandic. The twelve-volume edition *Íslendinga sögur* (1946–1947) is complete, containing all the Sagas of Icelanders and the *þættir* (see Chap. 3). The value of this edition is enhanced by the supplementary volume *Nafnaskrá*

(1949), which is the only complete index of saga place names and personal names extant. To date four volumes of the *Altnordische Textbibliothek* (1952–) have been published. The glossaries and excellent introductions to these editions make them suitable for independent study (see my review of the fourth volume in *Scandinavian Studies,* 1961). Scholar and layman alike will enjoy using the bilingual editions of the Nelson series (1957–). In addition to these collections, there are a number of splendid editions of individual sagas such as *Viga-Glúms saga* (2nd ed., 1960), edited by G. Turville-Petre, and *The Vinland Sagas* (1944), edited by Halldór Hermannsson. Two Sagas of Icelanders, *Gísla saga* and *Hrafnkels saga* appeared in the twelve-volume *Nordisk filologi* (1950–) series; they were edited by Agnete Loth and Jón Helgason, respectively.

The definitive edition of *Heimskringla* is that of Bjarni Aðalbjarnarson in the *Íslenzk fornit* series (Vols. 26–28; 1941–1951). The earlier Sagas of Kings are included in the three-volume edition *Konunga sögur* by Guðni Jónsson (1957). Jónsson has also edited the Sagas of Bishops (*Byskupa sögur*) and *Sturlunga saga* (2nd ed., 1953). Each of these comprises three volumes, which are supplemented by a seventh volume containing a common index. A critical edition of the Sagas of Bishops by Jón Helgason is in progress (1938–). The standard critical edition of *Sturlunga saga* is that of Jón Jóhannesson, Magnús Finnbogason, and Kristján Eldjárn (1946). One of the sagas of this compilation, *Þorgils saga ok Hafliða,* has appeared in two recent editions, by Halldór Hermannsson (1945) and by Ursula Brown (1952). The Sagas of Knights (*riddarasögur*) were published in six volumes by Bjarni Vilhjálmsson (1954). The mythical-heroic sagas (*fornaldarsögur*) were edited in three volumes by Guðni Jónsson and Bjarni Vilhjálmsson (1943–1944), and in six volumes by Jónsson (1949). For further editions of the sagas and for editions of Icelandic literature other than the sagas the reader is referred to the bibliographies listed below.

The critical literature on the sagas is so extensive as to be bewildering to the layman or beginning student in the field. The standard handbooks are, of course, indispensable but must be used with due consideration for their compilers' personal and national bias. Finnur Jónsson's monumental three-volume work, *Den oldnorske og oldislandske litteraturs historie* (2nd ed., 1924), contains a wealth of information. Unfortunately, however, the author was obsessed by the strange notion that the best of the Sagas of Icelanders were written at a very early period (before 1200), that few if any sagas were written during the thirteenth century, and that the stylistically inferior sagas were written after 1300. Jan de Vries' two-volume *Altnordische Literaturgeschichte* (1941–1942) is a work of great erudition which is marred by faulty method and highly subjective interpretation. An extensive treatment of the sagas is found in Frederik Paasche's *Norges og Islands litteratur inntil utgangen av middelalderen* (2nd ed., 1957). The value of this work is enhanced by the chapter supplements supplied by Anne Holtsmark in the second edition, which otherwise retains the original text of 1924. Of the older handbooks, the best by far is Jón Helgason's *Norrøn Litteraturhistorie* (1934), which was specifically designed for the use of university students. The presentation is concise, critical, and systematic. Andreas Heusler's views of the origin and transmission of the sagas can be read most conveniently in the second edition of his *Altgermanische Dichtung* (1941). Authoritative, up-to-date statements on individual sagas and the various genres of sagas are found in the *Kulturhistorisk leksikon for nordisk middelalder* (1956–), of which six volumes have appeared to date. More detailed and extensive treatments of various problems of saga research are found in some of the monographs of the four series *Bibliotheca Arnamagnæana, Is-*

landica, Studia Islandica (*Íslenzk fræði*), and *Saga.* The intriguing problem of the role of oral tradition in the Sagas of Icelanders is thoroughly treated in the monograph *Upphavet til den islendske ættesaga* (1929) by the eminent folklorist Knut Liestøl. This stimulating work is discussed in some detail by Hallberg (Chap. 5). As already mentioned in the Preface, the best historical survey of Old Icelandic prose literature is Sigurður Nordal's *Sagalitteraturen* (1953). Excellent literary and stylistic analyses of individual sagas are included in the introductions to many of the editions and translations discussed above. Especially important are those in Nordal's edition of *Egils saga* and E. Ó. Sveinsson's edition of *Njáls saga* in *Íslenzk fornrit.*

Lest the reader be discouraged at the large number of titles in Danish, Norwegian, Swedish, Icelandic, and German, I hasten to add that the number of scholarly works in English or English translation is also growing steadily. Stefán Einarsson's treatment of the sagas in his *History of Icelandic Literature* (1957) reflects the modern Icelandic point of view. *Origins of Icelandic Literature* (1953) by G. Turville-Petre is a thorough, perspicacious, well-documented account of the development of narrative prose composition, which represents one of the most significant original contributions yet made to our understanding of Old Icelandic literature. The final chapter of the book, which the author characterizes as an epilogue, presents a concise survey of the classical Sagas of Kings and Sagas of Icelanders. Of great value also is the monograph *Dating the Icelandic Sagas* (1959) by Einar Ólafur Sveinsson. This "essay in method" explains the criteria used in determining the relative chronology of the anonymous Sagas of Icelanders. Among older studies the most remarkable is the chapter "The Icelandic Sagas" by W. P. Ker in his well-known work *Epic and Romance* (1926). Bertha Phillpotts has also made some interesting comments on this genre in *Edda and Saga.* Despite its traditional slant, Sir William

Craigie's *The Icelandic Sagas* is useful for its lucid survey of the field and its concise summaries and characterizations of the most important individual works. Somewhat the same point of view is reflected by Halvdan Koht in his collection of essays *The Old Norse Sagas* (1930). The folkloristic study of Liestøl is available in English translation under the title *The Origin of the Icelandic Family Sagas* (1930). References to works on individual sagas or special problems are given in the notes.

The most detailed investigations of the Sagas of Kings are Bjarni Aðalbjarnarson, *Om de norske kongers sagaer* (1937) and Siegfried Beyschlag, *Konungasögur: Untersuchungen zur Königssaga bis Snorri* (1950). The introductions to the three volumes of Aðalbjarnarson's edition of *Heimskringla* are also very valuable. The pioneering work on the translated romances of chivalry is *Die Strengleikar* (1902) by R. Meissner, which, as the title indicates, deals chiefly with the Breton Lays. It is especially important for its stylistic analyses of these translations. The most thorough investigation of this genre is that of Henry Goddard Leach, *Angevin Britain and Scandinavia* (1921). Margaret Schlauch presents a detailed and comparative study of the late Icelandic sagas derived from the *riddarasögur* and the *fornaldarsögur* in her stimulating book *Romance in Iceland* (1934). A concise survey of the Sagas of Knights is given by E. F. Halvorsen in the introductory chapter of his monograph on *The Norse Version of the Chanson de Roland* (1959). Readers who are especially interested in the mythical-heroic sagas are referred to E. Ó. Sveinsson's condensed survey "Fornaldarsögur Norðurlanda" in the fourth volume of the *Kulturhistorisk leksikon* (1959), where the most important critical literature is cited.

The location of the extensive writings on Old Norse literature in general and on the Icelandic sagas in particular has been greatly facilitated by a number of bibliographies.

The most recent of these is *A Bibliography of Skaldic Studies* by L. M. Hollander (1958). Bibliographies of the *Eddas* have been published by Halldór Hermannsson (1920) and Jóhann S. Hannesson (1955). These also list editions, translations, and studies of the *Prose Edda* and the Grammatical Treatises (see Chap. 4). Hannesson's bibliography of *The Sagas of Icelanders* (1957) supplements two earlier bibliographies by Hermannsson (1908 and 1935). Since *Sturlunga saga*, the *þættir*, and the Sagas of Bishops all deal with native heroes, they, too, are in the broadest sense of the word "Sagas of Icelanders" and are therefore included here. The latest bibliography on *The Sagas of the Kings and the Mythical-heroic Sagas* was published by Hermannsson in 1937 as a supplement to his two previous bibliographies in this field (1910 and 1912). With the exception of Hollander's bibliography of skaldic studies, all of these bibliographies have appeared in the annual *Islandica*.

Of the various annual bibliographies, the most convenient for Americans are those found in *Scandinavian Studies* and the *Publications of the Modern Language Association*. The *Year's Work in Modern Language Studies* is also useful, although works on Icelandic, strangely enough, are listed under the rubric "Norwegian Literature." The most up-to-date bibliographies are those in the new quarterly *Germanistik* (1960–), which usually lists studies within six months of publication and includes short reviews of major works. For further annual bibliographies the reader is referred to the introductions to the bibliographies mentioned above.

Specialist and non-specialist alike will find the following bibliographical essays a welcome guide through the maze of scholarly and critical literature in the field. The most comprehensive work of this kind is Hermannsson's *Old Icelandic Literature* (1933). A concise survey of literary research in Iceland is afforded by Björn Sigfússon, "Islandsk

Litteraturforskning 1914–1938" and by Håkon Hamre, "Islandsk Litteraturforskning 1939–1947" in *Edda* (1940 and 1948). Stefán Einarsson discusses "Publications in Old Icelandic Literature and Language" in three papers of that title published in *Scandinavian Studies* (1938–1942). In another paper in that journal (1952) he reviews "Old Icelandic Literature: Editions in Iceland after 1940." The findings of the "Icelandic school" are discussed by Håkon Hamre in "Moderne islandsk sagagransking" in the journal *Syn og Segn* (1944). R. George Thomas' paper "Studia Islandica" published in two parts in the *Modern Language Quarterly* (1950) summarizes the chief contributions of Sigurður Nordal, especially during the years 1933–1941. The most detailed critical survey of modern saga research is Peter Hallberg, "Nyare Studier i den isländska sagan," *Edda,* 53 (1953), 219-247. My review of research in Old Norse literature since 1930 will appear in the forthcoming *MLA* handbook for students in medieval literature.

THE ICELANDIC SAGA

Introduction

As a LITERARY GENRE the Icelandic sagas dealing with native heroes—*Íslendingasögur*, "Sagas of Icelanders"—manifest a pronounced individuality. Without exaggeration they can be designated collectively as the sole original contribution of Scandinavia to world literature.

In choice of subject matter, in character portrayal, and in style these sagas are entirely and uniquely an Icelandic creation. They depict the immigration to Iceland, the occupation and settlement of the new country, viking expeditions, feuds among families and clans, and bitter legal disputes which pertained in considerable measure to property rights and personal prestige. The action of these stories takes place chiefly during the century following the establishment of the General Assembly in 930, the period which is generally called the Saga Age. The works themselves, however, were written much later; indeed, with few exceptions the central and classical works of this genre were produced in the thirteenth century. Although attempts have been made to identify the authors of some of the sagas with known historical personages, the creators of these renowned works are anonymous.

The Sagas of Icelanders have no counterpart either in the remaining countries of the North or in the rest of contemporary Europe. The complete absence of any definite points of contact with other literatures is striking. On the Continent the thirteenth century is the era of scholasticism with such great builders of philosophical systems as Albertus Magnus and Thomas Aquinas. Literature, too, to a high degree received its stamp from the Catholic faith, from the Christian concept of man. The allegory was diligently cultivated. Dante's *Divine Comedy*, the mighty crown of medieval poetry, is an artistically constructed

1

allegory. To a literature of this kind the Icelandic sagas of native heroes stand in marked contrast. As a rule they treat their matter in an extraordinarily objective and realistic manner, far removed from spiritualism and metaphysical brooding. The ideology which is delineated in the speech and actions of their characters is of pagan origin; the traces of Christian ethics are insignificant. Formally, at any rate, there prevails an almost complete freedom from moral value judgments. The saga observes a strict epic detachment; the narrator's ego is completely suppressed. This attitude of the writer toward his subject matter finds a fitting mode of expression in his unadorned and austere style.

The meaning of the word *saga* in Icelandic differs somewhat from that in English and the other Germanic languages. It refers to a narrative or account in general, often one with a purely historical content: *saga Íslands,* for example, means "the history of Iceland."[1] An animated discussion has revolved around the question of whether the Sagas of Icelanders should be regarded primarily as reliable family chronicles and histories or as fiction. Related to this problem is the question of the role played by oral tradition in their origin and transmission. On the one hand, the sagas are believed to be essentially historical: according to this theory they developed in close connection with the described events, were transmitted from generation to generation by storytellers, and were finally committed to parchment, generally sometime during the thirteenth century. Such an attitude toward the sagas scarcely permits one to talk about their authors; their writing would merely be a matter of recording a fixed oral tradition. On the other hand, they have been regarded by some scholars primarily as works of fiction. From this it naturally follows that one must accord to their writers a decisive role as true authors. These problems, which in one way or another arise in the study of much ancient and medieval epic literature, will be treated in a later chapter.

The Sagas of Icelanders have won fame not only as original narrative art. At various times they have also evoked intense interest as supposed history. Not least of all, they have been highly esteemed as a source of cultural history. In the profusion of saga characters the anonymous Icelandic masters have re-created the life of their forefathers in all its nuances, from the trivial cares of every day to great conflicts fraught with momentous consequences.

A literature of this kind requires a comparatively broad description of its general historical and cultural background. Among other things it is desirable from the very outset to gain an insight into certain administrative and juridical circumstances, peculiar to Iceland, which play a pervading and important role in the sagas.

CHAPTER 1

From the Settlement to
the Age of the Sturlungs

THE ICELANDERS are in the unusual position of having even
their genesis as a nation documented in writing. The remarkable record known as *Landnámabók* ("The Book of
the Settlements"), which may well have been compiled as
early as the twelfth century, mentions more than 3,000 persons and 1,400 places in connection with the colonization
of Iceland.[1]

The actual period of settlement is generally given as
870–930; by the turn of the century the coastal areas of the
country had for the most part been occupied. From all
indications, the driving force behind this immigration
seems to have been the policies of Haraldr hárfagri in Norway. According to tradition he is said to have crushed the
power of the regional kings and, to that end, to have de-
prived the farmers of their right to own their hereditary
lands (odal rights). Rather than submit to this new order,
many prominent men left Norway. A very large proportion
of them established new homes in Iceland, sometimes after
having spent several years in the Shetland Islands, the Orkneys, or the Hebrides, from where they set out on viking
expeditions. The areas which the leading settlers laid claim
to in the new country were not small plots of ground; they
were as extensive as modern Scandinavian parishes and
jurisdictional districts. Within these territories they ap-
portioned the land among their kinsmen and followers.

The settlers came to a practically untouched land. Those
people who had previously ventured there were very few in
number and had had an entirely different reason for doing

5

so than the Norse emigrants. The account in the Introduction to *Landnámabók* includes the following statement:

> But before Iceland was settled from Norway, there were men there whom the Norsemen call Papar. They were Christian, and it is thought that they had come from the British Isles, for people found after them Irish books, bells, and staffs and other objects from which it could be seen that they were men from the West.[2]

The memory of the *papar,* moreover, is still preserved in such place names as *Papey, Papóss, Papafjörður,* etc. It is evident that the *papar* were Irish monks or hermits who had decided to withdraw from the world and had found the island in the North Atlantic suited to their purpose. But they soon gave way, however, before the warlike pagan Norsemen.

But among the Norse settlers in Iceland there was also a considerable admixture of Celts from England, Scotland, Ireland, and the Hebrides. Probably these Celts were mostly thralls and captives whom the Norse immigrants brought along from their military expeditions.

This Celtic strain has played somewhat of a role in the discussion of the Icelanders' poetic art and narrative genius. Some people have believed that the artistic disposition of the Icelanders might have its foundation in this Celtic inheritance—a conjecture which, however, is scarcely worth discussing.

In the new country, of course, there soon arose a need for some sort of organization and for a forum for the discussion of common affairs. Consequently, in the year 930 the Icelandic General Assembly *(alþingi)* was established, with its meeting place at Þingvellir near the country's largest lake, Þingvallavatn. This is a region of unique and majestic natural beauty, with a magnificent view of the surrounding

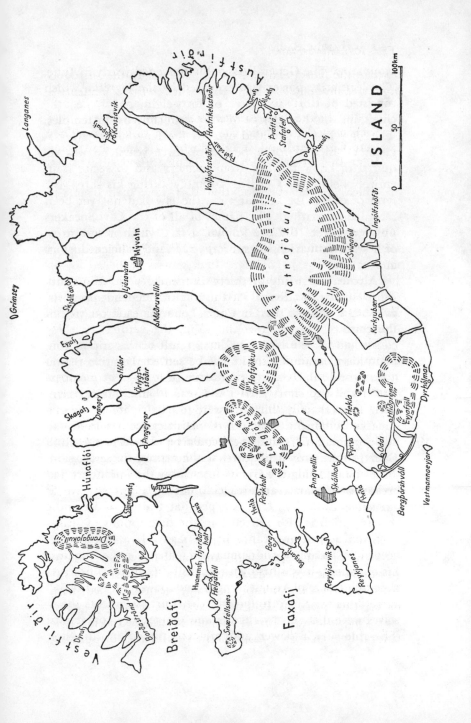

mountains. The General Assembly convened yearly in June. The legislative power was exercised by the *lögrétta,* which consisted of thirty-six, later of forty-eight, *goðar,* i.e., the chieftains who had charge of the pagan churches or temples. The *lögrétta* was presided over by the Law Speaker (*lögsö-gumaðr*). Elected for a period of three years, he was required to know the law from memory and to recite it in entirety before the General Assembly during his three-year term of office; for at that time the law had not yet been recorded in writing. The names of all of the Law Speakers up to the year 1272 are known, a fact which is indicative of how enviably rich the sources of Iceland's ancient history are.[3]

A court consisting of thirty-six members was also established. This was later divided into four independent courts, called District or Quarter Courts, one for each quarter of the country. In order to be valid, the verdicts of these courts had to be unanimous. As a result of this stipulation, many cases naturally could not be settled. For this reason a Fifth or High Court (*fimtardómr*) of forty-eight members was established shortly after the year 1000. Of these members, however, only thirty-six were to participate at any one time in judging a case. If the District Courts failed to achieve unanimity, an appeal could be carried to the High Court, where only a majority was necessary for a decision.

By establishing the General Assembly the Icelanders had created a legislative and judicial, but no administrative or executive authority. This is a peculiar feature of Icelandic society which is also reflected in the descriptions of litigation and acts of vengeance in the sagas. If a litigant succeeded in having a condemnatory sentence passed against his opponent, it was his own responsibility to execute it. As a consequence, of course, might and power in reality became decisive. Not infrequently the court judgments themselves were dictated by threats and peremptory commands. The role which power and violence played in litigation presents a sharp and strange contrast to the formalism and subtlety which were developed in legal procedure.

The lack of a central administrative and executive authority was to prove to be calamitous for Iceland's existence as an independent nation. It undermined the power of resistance to internal disintegration as well as to external pressures.

Every ninth farmer was obligated to accompany his *goði* to the General Assembly if the latter so desired. Those who remained at home had to pay the expenses of the Assembly participants. At the General Assembly the foremost men from all parts of the country met, and Þingvellir became an important center for the cultural life of the nation. Here an intensive activity unfolded, which was not restricted to official business. In their free time the young men competed in ball games, wrestling, and swimming. Beer parties were given for friends and acquaintances. Poets and storytellers contributed to the entertainment. From all indications the Assembly also played an essential role in the dissemination of news, perhaps also in a certain degree to the art of relating the news. There are various references to Icelanders who, having just returned home from abroad, related the "saga" of their travels at the Assembly.

As mentioned above, the *goðar* were the nucleus of the institution of the General Assembly. The title *goði* is derived from *goð* which means "(pagan) god"; and it will be remembered that the *goðar* also had charge of the temples. Besides their religious authority, however, they also had a secular one. Both their office and the domain of their power were designated by the term *goðorð*. In reality the godord was the only administrative unit of Iceland.[4] The godi was the chieftain of the district, and those who were subject to him were called his thingmen. The relationship between the godi and the thingmen, however, was quite free. The thingmen promised to accompany and support the godi, and in return he assured them of his protection. If they didn't get along, they could legally dissolve their mutual relationship. A farmer of one godord could seek the protection of the chieftain of another authority, i.e., he could "declare himself into the thing" of another godi; and each godi could accept anyone he wished into his "thing." The godord originally was thus not actually confined to a definitely bounded geographical district; it could perhaps best be characterized as a union of thingmen under the religious and secular leadership of a godi. This could, of course, increase or decrease according to the initiative and popularity of the individual godi. The godi with the greatest following was regarded as the most powerful and had the greatest influence; he could, if necessary, summon to arms the largest body of troops. The godord was hereditary, but it could also be sold, temporarily transferred, or divided and held in partnership.

Before the General Assembly in June the godar held the so-called spring assemblies at home on their godords. They cooperated in such a way that three authorities comprised one assembly or "thing."

It is especially interesting to follow the advance of Christianity and its clash with paganism. In this particular it should be possible to catch something of the spirit of the times, of man's view of his own position in the world and of his relationship to his fellow men.

Before Christianity was officially adopted in Iceland by decision of the General Assembly in the year 1000, there existed a condition of intermingling in the realm of creed and cult. Some of the original settlers were Christian; this is true especially of those who came to Iceland by way of the British Isles. But their zeal for the faith does not seem to have been overly strong. Concerning the settler Helgi inn magri, who was nominally Christian, *Landnámabók* states that he "had a mixed creed. He believed in Christ, but invoked the aid of Þórr before sea voyages and in difficult situations." On the other hand, the belief in the Æsir became watered down, and there were not a few who believed only *á mátt sinn ok meginn,* as the expression went, i.e., "in their own might and main." Association with Christians during travel abroad sometimes made it expedient for pagan Icelanders to have themselves prime-signed. This ceremony involved a sort of simple baptism: the sign of the cross was made over the pagans in order to drive out the evil spirits. *Egils saga Skalla-Grímssonar,* for example, relates that Egill and his brother Þórólfr, during their stay with the devout King Aðalsteinn (Ethelstan) in England, were admonished by him to let themselves be marked with the sign of the cross. "That was a common practice at that time both among merchants and among those who took service with Christian chieftains." Those who thus submitted to the *prima signatio* "could associate freely with both Christians and pagans, but held to that faith which was most in accordance with their minds."

Quite illuminating for the struggle between paganism and Christianity is the description of the relationship between King Ólafr Tryggvason and the skald Hallfreðr in the saga which bears that poet's name. King Ólafr, who was extremely zealous for the Christian faith, asked the recently arrived Hallfreðr to "renounce pagan ways and the evil faith," and to "serve the devil no longer," but rather "to believe in the true God, Creator of heaven and earth." Hallfreðr receives baptism with the king himself as his sponsor and is instructed in "sacred lore." But his later occasional poetry, recited before the king, reveals how difficult it was for him to make a complete break with his "pagan nature." In one of his verses he says: "All used to compose verses thus to gain the favor of Óðinn. I recall my forebears' praiseworthy lines, and reluctantly—for Óðinn's dominion pleased me—I turn against the husband of Frigg, because I serve Christ." It is not difficult to understand Hallfreðr's dilemma. In form and content the ancient skaldic poetry was deeply rooted in the cult of the Æsir and in the pagan view of life. To abjure completely these fundamental conditions and prerequisites meant for the skald the drying up of the very sources of his art.[5]

The Christian mission in Iceland is related in *Kristni saga* ("The History of Christianity"), which in its present form was written in the thirteenth century. The endeavor to convert Iceland was purposefully pursued by Óláfr Tryggvason, who probably was motivated by reasons other than purely religious ones. The Norwegian kings had for some time been reaching out their tentacles for Iceland, with the result that Iceland gradually came under the power of the Norwegian crown.

It was indeed a strange witness for the faith who was selected by Óláfr Tryggvason to convert Iceland. The man's name was Þangbrandr, and he was a German by birth. He had been forced to flee his native country because of manslaughter, landed at the court of King Óláfr, was ordained to the priesthood, and for a time served as the king's chaplain. Þangbrandr made some progress in his mission, but he also made enemies in Iceland. Several of these composed some scurrilous verses about him, to which he replied by killing them with his sword. In a similar manner he disposed of a berserker who had challenged him to a holmgang.[6] The result of this latter deed was immediate: several Icelanders let themselves be prime-signed.

Þangbrandr returned to Norway with the report that he had met with hostility in Iceland and that there was little likelihood that Christianity would be accepted there. King Óláfr became so angry at this that he ordered a number of Icelanders, who just happened to be in Norway at the time, to be seized and put in irons. He threatened to kill some and maim others of them. Two Christian Icelanders, Gizurr hvíti and Hjalti Skeggjason, interceded with the king by promising to advocate his cause in Iceland. But

Óláfr kept quite a few sons of prominent Icelanders as hostages until he learned the outcome of the matter.

Kristni saga gives a dramatic account of the conclusion of this struggle which was arrived at by the General Assembly in the year 1000. The disquieting dissension between pagans and Christians was resolved in a manner which gives evidence not so much of religious zeal on either side as of cool and moderate deliberation. The final decision was entrusted to Þorgeirr Ljósvetningagoði, who, himself a pagan, was among those who favored conciliation. He prepared himself for this task through a day of intensive concentration in the seclusion of his booth.[7] The following day he made a speech from the Law Rock in which he stated:

> I do not think it advisable to let those few men decide this issue who have here shown the greatest impetuousness. Let us rather mediate between the two parties in such a way that both of them will realize their desires in some measure. But let us all have one law and one faith, for it will prove to be true that if we divide the law, we will also destroy the peace.

Both parties agreed to abide by Þorgeirr's solution. Thereupon he determined

> that all people in Iceland were to be baptized and believe in one God; but in regard to the exposure of children and the eating of horsemeat, the old law was to remain in effect. People should be permitted to hold pagan sacrificial feasts in secret if they wished to, but under penalty of the lesser outlawry if this were discovered.[8]

A provision such as that relating to pagan sacrifice, to be sure, reveals very little of the spirit of Christianity. The point of view is conventional and social; one was not to give offense to others by his heathen practices. The entire manner in which Christianity was introduced seems to indicate that religion was regarded essentially as a community affair

rather than as a matter of personal conviction. The indifference toward religion takes on an almost comical aspect
in the description of the collective baptism following the
conclusion of the General Assembly. *Kristni saga* relates
that the thingmen from the North and South Quarters were
baptized in the warm spring Reykjalaug in Laugardalr on
their way home from the Assembly because they did not
want to go into the cold water at Þingvellir.

During its earliest period the Icelandic church was quite
different from the Catholic church on the Continent, not
least of all in its relationship to secular power. The church
in Iceland was far from enjoying the same independent position as a sort of state within a state with legislative and
judicial authority in its own affairs. All changes in ecclesiastical law, all new regulations regarding the clergy, had to
be submitted to the legislative branch of the assembly
(*lögrétta*), where, like all other legal questions, they were
decided by the goðar. The spring assemblies and the General Assembly exercised judicial power in ecclesiastical as
well as in secular matters; and the clergy, no less than their
fellow countrymen, were subject to the laws then in force.

The unique position of the Icelandic church is closely
connected with its origin. Apparently the church replaced
the old pagan temples without much friction and also took
over some of their traditions. Here again the lack of a
central administrative state power is evident. The churches
were built by individual farmers or chieftains on their own
farms. The church building thus became the private property of the individual farmer, and this situation did not
change if the farmer was also the priest of the church, as
was sometimes the case. The parish priest himself collected
the tithes and certain other taxes, in return for which he
held divine services and provided for the upkeep of the
building.

The clerical office itself could be filled in three different
ways. The church owner could undertake the duty himself

if he had sufficient education. There are many instances of chieftains who had themselves ordained and continued to rule their godord. Some of these also engaged in seafaring and trade or in other activities which do not seem quite appropriate for the incumbent of a divine office. Such godord priests figured prominently in feuds and manslaughter suits, both on their own account and in support of relatives and friends. Others realized the awkwardness of such a conflict of interests and preferred to transfer the godord to relatives in order to be able to devote themselves completely to their ecclesiastical duties.

Another way of providing for priestly services was to employ a priest, called a "hired priest" *(leiguprestr)*, for a fixed annual salary which amounted to one-fourth of the tithe. Such a priest was employed for a year at a time, just like the other servants, and the farmer who owned the church had to provide him with board and room.

The third possibility was this: the farmer could have a young man trained to be priest of his church—a *prestlingr*, as the adept was called. The farmer was obliged to make a contract with the youth himself, or with his guardian, and to provide him with all the training and education he needed until he was ordained. Thereafter the *prestlingr*, who was also called a church priest, was bound to his church like a thrall. If he ran away from the church he had been trained for, the farmer could announce that fact at the General Assembly, forbid people to associate with him just as though he were an outlaw, and demand the return of his priest just like any other runaway thrall. The only possibility a church priest had of escaping from this bond service was to train someone else to take his place.

This dependence of the priesthood on secular power is certainly one important reason why the church never got the same firm hold on the nation as in other countries. On the other hand, it may be that the position of the Icelandic priests was partly responsible for the fact that in Iceland there did not develop any real schism between the servants of the church and the common man.

An episcopal see was established at Skálholt in the South around the middle of the eleventh century, and a second one at Hólar in the North at the beginning of the twelfth century. The first bishop at Hólar, Jón Ögmundarson, is said to have founded an excellent school there and to have appointed foreign teachers in Latin, music, and poetic composition. It was on his initiative, too, that the first monastery was founded at Þingeyrar. The Icelandic monasteries, especially the one at Þingeyrar, played an important role in the recording of popular tradition from pagan times. This reveals a tolerant and unprejudiced attitude that may be attributed to the national character of the Icelandic church.

Sometimes the sagas give clear evidence of the manner in which a scribe or author tried to create a synthesis of his own Christian faith and the traditional pagan view of life. Some manuscripts of *Fóstbrœðra saga,* which is considered to be one of the oldest of the extant sagas, show a very striking Christian influence. This conflicts with the ancient hero-ideal, which is just as vigorously asserted, in a way that brings a smile to the modern reader. A good example is the following statement about one of the sworn-brothers, Þorgeirr, who as a youth has killed his father's slayer:

> All who heard this news thought it a remarkable deed that such a young man should have slain so powerful a chieftain and so great a warrior as Jöðurr. And yet this was not strange. For the Creator of the world had formed and placed in Þorgeirr's breast so fierce and fearless a heart that he could not be afraid, but was as dauntless as a lion in all tests of courage. And since all good things have been created by God, so, too, fearlessness was created by God and put into the breast of courageous men and thus also the freedom and strength to do as they will, whether that be good or evil. For

Christ has made Christians His sons and not His thralls, and He will reward each one according to his merits. (Chap. 3.)

This line of reasoning recalls a statement made by Laxness in 1945 in an essay on the sagas: that although heathendom and Christendom long had existed side by side in Iceland, these two ways of faith and life could never be united with each other any more than cold water and molten lead.[9]

CHAPTER 2

The Age of the Sturlungs and the Fall of the Commonwealth

DURING THE ELEVENTH CENTURY things seem to have been relatively quiet in the Icelandic community. But in the twelfth century strife and violence flared up and became increasingly more serious in the course of the following century. This era, from the middle of the twelfth century until the fall of the Commonwealth in 1262, is usually called the Age of the Sturlungs, after one of the predominant families.

At first glance it may seem farfetched to dwell at some length on the Sturlung Age in connection with the Sagas of Icelanders. The events which these sagas reflect belong, after all, to the "Saga Age" which was several centuries earlier. But the matter of the sagas is one thing, and their literary development and formation is quite another. And the writing of these works, as already mentioned, took place mostly during the thirteenth century, that is, during and shortly after the Sturlung epoch. Furthermore, it is a controversial question as to what extent the sagas give us a reasonably reliable picture of the Saga Age and to what degree they reflect the spirit and the conditions of the time in which they were written. Quite recently, in fact, an Icelandic scholar dared go so far as to interpret *Njála*, the most famous of the Sagas of Icelanders, as a *roman à clef* from the Sturlung Age.[1] He concluded that a definite author with a definite purpose had depicted in the characters and episodes of this saga certain persons, including himself, as well as events from his own time. However one may feel about the correctness of this interpretation of *Njála*, it is clear, in any event, that it is based on a completely reasonable principle. It seems logical to assume that the sagas in their present form must have received a decisive impression from the time in which they were written. And this means, of course, that the Sturlung Age is of the greatest interest and importance for students of the sagas of Icelandic heroes.[2]

By a fortunate circumstance one can read about the Sturlung Age in a unique, detailed, contemporary work. This is *Sturlunga saga,* called *Sturlunga* for short, a composite document which describes the history of Iceland during the twelfth and thirteenth centuries.[3] This compilation consists of a number of loosely connected "sagas." The treatment of the first half of the thirteenth century, which comprises a large and essential portion of the work, is by Sturla Þórðarson (1214–1284), a nephew of Snorri Sturluson and himself involved in violent factional struggles in Iceland. He must, therefore, have been in an exceptionally good position to give a realistic and vivid picture of his time. One would scarcely expect, to be sure, that this picture would be completely objective in every respect. And yet, light and shadow are distributed with astonishing equality over the opposing parties in spite of the wild and turbulent times which are described here. The respect of the old Icelandic historians for cold facts, it seems, was firmly entrenched from the days of Sæmundr fróði and Ari fróði.[4]

First of all, the political development during the Sturlung Age will be sketched here. In the following chapter several striking features of the general physiognomy of that epoch will be scrutinized.

After the middle of the twelfth century the balance of power among the godar began to be disturbed. With increasing frequency individual chieftains gained control of more than one godord. In part this was due to the fact that a considerable number of chieftains who had been ordained as priests relinquished their godord authorities in order to avoid, as much as possible, becoming involved in secular feuds. This was a tendency which was strongly supported by the church. Finally the old social structure was completely disrupted: in place of many godar with approximately equal power, there were a few energetic and influential individuals and families who subjected large parts of the country to their control. Among these chieftains there raged uninterrupted conflicts, which reached their culmination in the early decades of the thirteenth century and eventually led to the submission of Iceland to the rule of the Norwegian king.

The greatest interest among the feuding families centers upon the Sturlungs themselves, who have given their name to the entire period. The founder of this clan was Sturla Þórðarson (1115–1183), called Hvamm-Sturla after his farm Hvammur in the Hvammsfjörður. He is not to be confused with the historian Sturla, his grandson and namesake, who lived just a hundred years later. Like certain other chieftains of his day, Hvamm-Sturla was an upstart. But he more than made up for his lack of pedigree through ambition, cunning, and ruthlessness; and he gradually became the most powerful and influential man in the western districts.

The family's real period of power began with Hvamm-Sturla's sons, Þórðr, Sighvatr, and Snorri. Snorri Sturluson (1179–1241), who was the youngest of the brothers, gained fame not only as a historian and poet. He was also successful in more mundane affairs. Thanks among other things to his two well-calculated marriages, he was able to achieve great prestige and wealth. He visited Norway, where he gained the favor of both King Hákon Hákonarson and Jarl Skúli. He even succeeded in averting a Norwegian military expedition against Iceland by himself promising to plead the king's cause among his countrymen. Little came of this mission, however, after he had once returned home. In 1222 Snorri was elected Law Speaker for the second time, and during the following years he reached the peak of his power, in part at the expense of his own kinsmen. He was especially unscrupulous in his treatment of his brother Sighvatr and his brother's son Sturla.

And yet it was precisely this man, Sturla Sighvatsson, who was to bring the political influence of the Sturlungs to its first culmination. Before this, Sturla figures prominently in an interlude which in a unique manner reflects the wild manner in which accounts were settled in Iceland. He and his father had been guilty of an aggression against the renowned Bishop Guðmundr Arason (1160–1237), called the Good. Sturla made a pilgrimage to Rome for the purpose of receiving absolution from the pope himself. *Sturlunga* relates the following concerning this incident:

> In Rome Sturla received absolution from all his and his father's transgressions and submitted there to a severe penance. He was led barefoot from one church to another throughout the city and was chastized in front of most of the cathedrals. He bore this manfully, as was to be expected; but throngs of people stood outside and marveled and lamented the fact that such a handsome man should be so ill-treated, and they could not hold back their tears, neither men nor women. (II, 97.)

After this voyage of penance Sturla paid a visit to Norway. King Hákon expressed the opinion that the best way to put an end to the strife in Iceland would be to introduce absolute monarchy there. Sturla undertook—in return for the bestowal of suitable honors—to work for the king's cause. But he was constrained not to win the country with bloodshed; rather, he was to seize his adversaries and send them abroad or else to subjugate them and confiscate their estates in some other way. When Sturla returned home, he first turned against his uncle, Snorri Sturluson, and the latter's son Órækja. In accordance with the king's instructions, Snorri was driven away from his stronghold in the Borgarfjörður District and finally was forced into exile.

The ambitious and ruthless Sturla met his doom at the hands of two young chieftains, Gizurr Þorvaldsson (1208–

1268 and Kolbeinn Arnórsson the Young (1208–1245). Under the pretext of wanting to make an alliance with Gizurr, Sturla treacherously got him into his power, extorted from him a promise that he would leave the country, and made him swear an oath of fealty to him. Naturally, Gizurr never intended to keep his oath, which was given under duress. He joined forces with Kolbeinn the Young and with an army of 1,700 men defeated Sturla and his father Sighvatr at Örlyggsstaðir in the summer of 1238 in the largest pitched battle ever fought in Iceland. Both father and son were slain after a brave defense.

Peace and quiet, however, were not restored in Iceland through this. After the battle at Örlyggsstaðir Snorri Sturluson and Óraekja returned from exile and attempted to regain their former position of political power. But in this situation Gizurr Þorvaldsson and Kolbeinn the Young had a strong trump card to play, for King Hákon had written to Gizurr and ordered him either to get Snorri out of the country or to kill him. In this letter the king accused Snorri of high treason. Obviously he was displeased with Snorri for the manner in which he had espoused the royal cause in Iceland; from all indications Snorri had not been overly energetic in carrying out this mission.

On the authority of the king's letter, Gizurr and Kolbeinn the Young had Snorri murdered one night in September, 1241, on his estate at Reykholt. It is quite consonant with the prevailing conditions of that time in Iceland that both Gizurr and Kolbeinn were sons-in-law of the slain; they had formerly been married to daughters of Snorri.

It is not necessary here to discuss the various phases of the last two decades of the Icelandic Commonwealth. Among the prominent men beside Gizurr and Kolbeinn who played important roles in the final period one may mention Þórðr Sighvatsson kakali (1210–1256) and Þorgils Böðvarsson skarði (1226–1258), both of them members of the Sturlung clan. Þórðr was a brother of Sturla Sighvatsson but had escaped sharing his brother's and father's fate at Örlyggsstaðir because he was in Norway at that time. The Norwegian king's hold on Iceland became stronger and stronger. After the death of Snorri Sturluson the king had his property and chieftaincy confiscated. Icelandic chieftains voluntarily relinquished their godord authorities to the king. In their internal disputes they sought the support of the king and appealed to him to decide the issues. The outcome of all this was that the Icelanders swore loyalty and homage to the King of Norway and became tributary to the Norwegian crown (1262–1264). From that time on, Iceland had a foreign ruler until, almost seven hundred years later, the Republic was proclaimed at Þingvellir on June 17, 1944.

CHAPTER 3

General Characteristics
of the Sturlung Age

IN THE PRECEDING CHAPTER the external contours of the turbulent course of political events during the Sturlung Age were briefly sketched. But more essential as a background for the literary creativity of the time are the prevailing manner of thinking and the view of life which determined men's actions. In this point, too, *Sturlunga* is an extraordinarily rich source of information.

The relations between the leading men of Iceland and the Norwegian king reveal a good deal about the Icelandic attitude toward personal and national independence. Many Icelandic chieftains became liegemen of the king during their visits to Norway; Gizurr Þorvaldsson was actually made an earl over Iceland and surrounded himself with his own retinue. The power of resistance of such men was consequently not so strong when the king proposed that they should work for his cause in their native country; by doing so they would, after all, be serving their own ends in their struggle for power. And yet, almost without exception, they carried out the king's mission with an extraordinary lack of enthusiasm when they did return to Iceland. Obviously they had a certain aversion to their commission, and a feeling that it was not very popular among their fellow countrymen. Prominent Icelanders were, therefore, summoned to Norway time after time to account for the insignificant or nonexistent results of their efforts in the king's service.

One of the chieftains who had personal reasons for giving serious thought to the state of affairs between the Icelanders and the royal power of Norway was Snorri

Sturluson. And from his writings one can see how strongly this problem occupied him, especially during the decade following his return home in the king's commission. Of especial interest and significance in this connection is the long section in *Óláfs saga helga* that Snorri took from the history of the Faroe and Orkney Islands, which is a discussion of their relations with the Norwegian king. The central portion is Snorri's report of Óláfr Haraldsson's message to the General Assembly. Since this passage has become classical in Iceland as an expression of the Icelandic attitude toward the royal power and as a symbol of the Icelandic will to resist foreign subjugation, it will be discussed briefly here.

By way of introduction Snorri names several prominent Icelanders who became vassals of King Óláfr and tells about the exchange of gifts between the king and them. "But," adds Snorri, "in these tokens of friendship which the king showed Iceland there was a deeper significance, as has since then come to light." Óláfr had sent over an Icelander by the name of Þórarinn Nefjólfsson, who conveyed to the General Assembly God's and Óláfr's greetings as well as Óláfr's willingness to be king of the Icelanders if they desired to become his subjects. This speech was well received, and all declared that they would gladly be friends of the king if he were a friend of the Icelanders. Then Þórarinn went on with his speech and said that the king requested as evidence of the friendship of the people of the North Quarter the island or "outlying skerry" Grímsey, north of Eyjafjörður. In the following deliberations the influential chieftain Guðmundr of Möðruvellir spoke in favor of acceding to the king's request, and many agreed with him. Then someone asked why Guðmundr's brother Einarr did not express an opinion. Einarr began to speak:

> The reason I have said little about this matter is that no one asked me to do so. But if I am to state my opinion, I believe it would be best for our people not

25

to submit to paying taxes to King Óláfr and all those other tributes such as he demands from the people in Norway. We would be inflicting this bondage not upon ourselves alone, but upon both us and our sons and all our kin who will dwell in this land. And the yoke would never disappear or be lifted from our country.

Even if this king be a good man, as I well believe he is, nevertheless it will happen in the future as it has in the past with the succession of kings, that they are not alike, some being good men and others evil. And if our countrymen wish to retain their freedom, which they have had ever since this land was settled, they must beware of giving the king a foothold, whether in the form of land ownership here or of fixed payment of tribute from here which could be regarded as a subject tax. On the other hand, I think it proper that those who wish to do so send the king gifts of friendship, such as hawks or horses, tents or sails, or other things which are fitting to be given. For these things are well spent if they bring friendship in return.

But in regard to Grímsey it should be said that if no stores of food are carried away from that place, then an army can be fed there. And if there is a foreign army there, and it sets out from there in longships, then, I think, many a small farmer will find himself hard pressed. (Chap. 125.)

After Einarr's speech the Assembly voted unanimously to reject the king's proposition.

It is scarcely possible that Snorri could have created such a scene from his country's history two hundred years previously without having the conditions of his own time in mind. Something similar must be true of the anonymous writers of the sagas of native heroes. Suspicion against the monarchy was deeply rooted in Iceland. According to tradition, it will be remembered, the very origin of the Icelandic nation was due to the unwillingness of the early settlers to submit to the new order of Haraldr hárfagri. To the Icelanders of the Sturlung Age the Norwegian king represented a foreign threat, a superior power, to which, without the most heroic resistance, one would finally have to submit. It is reasonable to assume that the saga writers should reveal a certain tendency to picture their forefathers as more stiff-necked than the Icelanders of their own day, as more equal parties in their dealings with the king. But one must not simply consider it as an idealization of distance and time when frank, undaunted behavior before the king finds striking expression in the sagas. One must also take into consideration the fact that relations between free individuals and the king during an earlier period actually were more informal. During the thirteenth century the monarchy had developed to the point where it could surround itself with more complex ceremony, and then its contact with the common man was no longer so direct.

None of the major Sagas of Icelanders gives such a fresh and finely shaded description of the relations of an individual man or family to the Norwegian king as *Egils saga Skalla-Grímssonar*. In this account of the strife between the family of Kveld-Úlfr and that of the king, one can distinguish two different strains or tendencies which correspond quite well to the two diverse personality types within Kveld-Úlfr's own family. One of them is represented by the two Þórólfrs: Kveld-Úlfr's son and grandson, the former the uncle of the latter. In appearance and bearing they are splendid figures, great warriors conscious of their own worth yet devoid of all barbaric traits. They are attracted to the royal court and are, with their appreciation of chivalric manners and customs, obviously cut out to be liegemen of the king. Kveld-Úlfr himself, together with his son Skalla-Grímr and grandson Egill, represent another line in the family. Even in outward appearance these men differ radically from the two Þórólfrs. In their hugeness of body and their uncommon facial features they all bear the mark of trolls or giants—a word which is once actually used in reference to Skalla-Grímr. In their very nature they have a

27

wild and demonic element which finds expression in the
fury of the berserker, in the supernatural gift of second
sight, and in magical arts. They are extreme individualists,
impossible to discipline. It is this trait in their characters
which brings about the serious clashes with the king and
precludes all possibility of a reconciliation.

The author of *Egils saga*—with good reason one has con-
jectured that he was Snorri Sturluson himself, Egill's great
descendant—has thus within the framework of one and the
same family reflected the many and varied relations between the king and individual freemen. This is a subject
which in itself must have been of tremendous interest for
the Icelanders of the Sturlung Age. But it is not a question
of a direct projection of contemporary problems into an
earlier era. The social and legal point of view, which must
have been of primary importance in the relationship of the
Icelanders to the royal house during the thirteenth century,
is scarcely noticeable in the saga. Instead, everything is intensely personal, a series of dramatic clashes and conflicts
between distinctive individuals. Perhaps, as already indicated, the saga reflects the more direct dealings of a
former time between the king and the private individual.
But it is most probable that tradition and the saga writer
have endowed their Icelandic heroes with more imposing
dimensions than would be revealed by sober reality. For
the people in the oppressed nation of the Sturlung Age it
must have been comforting and exemplary to see their
ancestors frankly and fearlessly come before the king and
assert their rights and personalities in defiance of him.

Quite a few *þættir* treat in the *novella* form various
episodes involving the Norwegian king and an Icelander.
As an example, one could choose the *þáttr* about Stúfr, who
had sailed to Norway to collect a legacy.[1] He took lodging
with a farmer, and they had just sat down to eat their meal
when King Haraldr harðráði with a large body of men
arrived there for a visit. The farmer arose from the table

at once and told all the people to leave, since the king had come. All removed themselves except the Icelander, who calmly remained sitting. At first Stúfr appears to be a yokel who is completely lacking in good manners in social intercourse with royalty. But, at the same time, his slow and easy composure contrasts in a humorous and not unattractive way with the farmer's officious zeal in clearing the seats and benches for the king and his retinue. King Haraldr's first impression of Stúfr seems to have been that he was a somewhat boorish and simple fellow who could be a suitable butt for their jests. But, bit by bit, the Icelander reveals as a counterpart to his lack of courtly polish a certain native soundness of reasoning, a straightforwardness, and a ready wit, which win the king's admiration. And when the narrator finally takes leave of Stúfr, it is with the comment that he was thought to be "a wise and popular man."

Both in *Egils saga* and in *Stúfs þáttr* one meets various shades of the old Icelandic individualistic and democratic spirit. That a man like Egill with his highly respected family and influential friends to support him should regard himself as the king's equal and demand an eye for an eye is perhaps not so surprising. More noteworthy is the fact that Stúfr in such a matter-of-fact manner should assert his individuality in the presence of Haraldr harðráði. In the description of such characters there is revealed a pronounced interest in the individual regardless of his social position. This is an attitude which can reasonably be expected to take root among a people of such small numbers with no real class differences—except for that between free men and thralls—and without a sovereign authority walled around by symbols of power.

The same individualism and self-assertion which, according to the testimony of the sagas, characterized the Icelander of the time of the Commonwealth in his relationship to the Norwegian king, also mark his reaction to peremptory commands of the church. When the powerful bishop Þorlákr Þórhallsson (d. 1193) ordered the chieftains to relinquish their churches—the Icelandic churches, as previously mentioned, were from the outset the property of the "church farmers"—and in support of this cited the messages of the pope and the archbishop, he encountered tenacious resistance from several men, including the highly esteemed Jón Loftsson (d. 1197): "I can hear the message of the archbishop, but I am determined not to pay any regard to it, for I do not believe that his will or knowledge is better than that of my forefathers, Sæmundr inn fróði and his sons." When the same bishop Þorlákr tried to separate Jón Loftsson from his companion or concubine, who moreover was the bishop's own sister, and threatened to excommunicate him, Jón is said to have replied:

> I know that your ban is legitimate, and that the cause is sufficient. I shall comply with your request in this way: I shall go to Þórsmörk or some other place where people will not incur any guilt from associating with me and live there with the woman for whose sake you are proceeding against me as long as it pleases me. But neither your interdict nor the coercion of any other man will separate me from my difficulties until God breathes into my breast that I should give them up of my own free will.[2]

It is obvious that such a mentality stands in sharp opposition to the attitude preached by the church. Jón relied entirely on his own judgment, with his forebears as a moral support. But this unbridled individualism, this defiant assertion of one's own ego must from the point of view of the church have appeared like a dangerous survival of the old pagan faith in one's own might and main. It lay within the interests of the church to strengthen the concept among the people that man was nothing in and of himself, that he had value only as a member of the holy general church. But this was an idea that was as foreign as possible to the ancient Icelandic view of life, in which the virtue of humility was not highly regarded. Even the demands of discipline and the need for organization must have been difficult to accept in a society which from the very beginning lacked an executive power and in which the individual free man had so much elbowroom.

The Sturlung Age enjoys a firm reputation for barbaric immorality. It is not merely the devastating internal feuds as such which have given the era that name but also certain striking traits, like deceit and savagery, which have been relentlessly recorded in *Sturlunga saga*. Even among close relatives within the families of prominent men amity is extremely fragile; one need think only of Sturla's sons. Time after time there are reports of forged letters sent out to entice one's enemy to destruction. The breaking of promises is common. There are instances of chieftains who have the men of their adversaries maimed: a hand or foot is cut off, or they are castrated. The practice of having concubines was widespread, even among the clergy, and evoked bitter complaints from the church leadership about immoral ways of life.

On the other hand, an Icelandic scholar has asserted that the Sturlung Age was scarcely any worse morally than any other epoch. It has merely paid the penalty for having received such a stern and detailed chronicle in *Sturlunga saga*. And in other countries, with their more complex and large-scale social conditions, the powers that be, and subsequently the historians, could mask their acts of violence as a political necessity, depict them as a more or less legal punishment. "But here in Iceland one scarcely applies the concept of the state to mere individuals. It is they who must shoulder the full responsibility for their deeds."[3]

And yet one gains a definite impression that even the manner of armed combat suffered a certain deterioration since the time of the sagas, at least to the extent that the Saga Age is realistically reflected in literature. As an example, one might refer to the description of the death of Sighvatr and Sturla in the battle at Örlyggsstaðir.

Sighvatr had withdrawn from the fight with several followers and had remained lying on the ground. He was not seriously wounded, but he was a man of sixty-seven and was quite exhausted. Several opponents, among them Kolbeinn the Young himself, used weapons against him as he lay defenseless. They stripped the slain man of all of his clothing except his shirt and underpants.

While this incident was taking place, Sighvatr's son Sturla was fighting for his life on another part of the battlefield. A small man whom he had just knocked down with a blow of his sword had got to his feet again and gave him a spear thrust through the right cheek. And then he got two more wounds. Hjalti biskopsson pierced his left cheek so that the spear point cut through the tongue and entered the bone. Someone else thrust his spear through his throat and up into the mouth. Then Sturla called out to Hjalti biskopsson: "Peace, kinsman!" "You shall have peace as far as I am concerned," replied Hjalti. They both withdrew from the fighting. Weariness and loss of blood had sapped Sturla's strength; Hjalti laid an arm around him and supported him.

But they hadn't gone very far before Sturla threw himself down on the ground. He could no longer speak clearly; Hjalti thought he heard him ask for a priest, and he went to fetch one. Some other men remained with Sturla; one of them placed a shield over him, and another one a small buckler. Then Gizurr Þorvaldsson himself came there. He tore away the protective shields and also Sturla's helmet and said only these words: "This is my business." He took a broad-bladed axe from the hands of one of the men and struck Sturla in the head with it behind the left ear. Those who were present related afterward that Gizurr jumped up in the air when he brandished the axe and hewed with it so that one could see between the soles of his shoes and the ground. One man thrust Sturla through the throat and up into the mouth in the same wound he had received before so that now one could stick three fingers through it. Another one pushed his sword into Sturla's abdomen, above and to the right of the navel. A third man struck him in the throat with his axe. Then the fallen chieftain's body was plundered until it lay there naked.[4]

Sturla Þórðarson was certainly not governed by any desire to idealize when he wrote his report of the battle at Örlyggsstaðir. One seeks in vain in the Sagas of Icelanders for anything remotely approaching these revolting details. Here in *Sturlunga* the fighting is more petty, but at the same time more cruel. No powerful death-dealing blows are exchanged, no heads are split down to the shoulder at a single stroke. The assailant picks and pokes cautiously with his weapons, and his courage rises in proportion to his adversary's defenselessness and seems to reach its climax when he is dead. Sighvatr and Sturla suffer their death-blows as they lie on the ground completely helpless. Gizurr's awkward caper as he swings his axe at Sturla is nothing less than ludicrous. When one reads this authentic contemporary report by an eyewitness, one has a strong impression that the battle descriptions in the classical sagas must have represented something belonging to the far distant past for the Icelanders of the Sturlung Age. And at any rate one at least has the right to raise the question whether the sagas' heroic ideals and warrior-ethics were not in essence the fond dream and idealized fiction of a later epoch rather than the depiction of a once-existing reality.

The tendency toward dissolution and the lack of a moral focus during the Sturlung Age have been interpreted in part as a result of the tension between paganism and Christianity. This does not hold true in regard to religious forms and customs. As a cult, paganism had been abolished; certainly no one indulged secretly in pagan sacrifice in Snorri Sturluson's time. But the opposition and contrast are revealed in the people's view of life. The old pagan ideal of pride, independence, and self-esteem, which plays such an important role in the culture of ancient Iceland, contrasts sharply with the Christian dogma of man's insignificance and perdition. The old individualism persisted tenaciously, and through the social development in Iceland it had come to lack the necessary counterweight in family solidarity and a feeling of social responsibility, and so it had degenerated among certain powerful men into complete ruthlessness. After men had halfheartedly given up the ancient standard of values without having completely acquired the new norms of Christianity, they could easily slide into a state of disorientation and uncertainty in the moral evaluation of human actions.

It was in such an atmosphere, then, that the Icelandic sagas of native heroes were written. They comprise, moreover, merely one branch of the rich literary production of Iceland during the twelfth and thirteenth centuries. The following chapter will give a sketch of the prose literature of the period in its entirety.

CHAPTER 4

Survey of the Literature of Iceland in the Twelfth and Thirteenth Centuries

IN ICELAND the use of the vernacular for written records began around the year 1100. In any event, this happened not later than the winter of 1117/1118, when portions of the laws were written down; it will be remembered that before this time it was the duty of the Law Speaker to preserve the laws by memory. The so-called *First Grammatical Treatise*, which is generally dated around 1150, confirms the fact that reading and writing had become common in Iceland by that time.[1] This work specifically mentions several branches of literature which were already being cultivated in the Icelandic language: laws, genealogical records, interpretations of sacred writings, and "the historical lore which Ari Þorgilsson has recorded in his books with discretion and intelligence"—i.e., Ari's historical works. At the outset, then, the art of writing in the vernacular was made to serve a useful purpose in recording the results of investigation and works of edification; it was not used for the purpose of entertainment. But even in these practical, matter-of-fact forms Icelandic prose could contribute considerable material and certain models of style to the composition of sagas.[2]

In a homogeneous, exclusively rural society like that of medieval Iceland, family traditions are usually very strong. This naturally must have been especially pronounced in a nation of emigrants, in which the very act of transplantation to a new country intensified the interest in the relationships within and among the various families and in their origin and ancestors.³ At the beginning of the twelfth century people in Iceland were busily occupied with the recording of their genealogies. In part this was probably a purely practical matter. In certain legal questions which concerned the family—compensation for manslaughter, rights of inheritance, responsibility and claims for support, etc.—genealogical lists were almost indispensable, for kinship even down to remote generations was taken into consideration. As is well known, the writers of sagas of native heroes made zealous use of such genealogical lists. Often this was done in order to lend the story a desired air of historical authenticity; sometimes it was for the purpose of providing the chief characters with illustrious ancestors. Undeniably these family trees often seem dull and boring to the modern reader. Yet they cannot simply be disregarded, since, thoughtfully read, they sometimes furnish the key to the characters' position in a conflict.

The genealogies are of especial significance in *Landnámabók*, which lists about four hundred of the most prominent original settlers around the entire coast of Iceland and indicates where they came from, where they settled, to whom they were married, and who their descendants were. Not much is known about the origin of this book. Obviously, however, its genesis must be sought in the genealogical lists compiled in the first half of the twelfth century. *Landnámabók* itself refers to persons who supplied information about families and "land-takes" in various parts of the country. Portions of the book consist of laconic and dry listings of names of persons and places. But ever and again there are also strewn in vivid descriptions of situations which sometimes can assume the sharp contours of dramatic episodes in the style of the sagas. One such passage tells about a son who opposed the remarriage of his widowed mother and slew her suitor. The latter's son in turn fell upon his father's slayer and killed him:

Þorgrímr grew fond of Áshildr after the death of
Óláfr, but Helgi opposed this. He waited for Þorgrímr
by a fork in the road below Áshildarmýrr. Helgi asked
him to stop his visits. Þorgrímr declared he was not a
child. They fought. Þorgrímr fell there. Áshildr asked
Helgi where he had been. He recited a verse.
(In the verse Helgi triumphantly says that the sword-
blades rang out loudly, that he made the attack and gave
the bold son of Þormóðr to Óðinn and a corpse to the
ravens.) Áshildr said that he had struck his own deathblow.
Helgi tried to get to Einarshöfn in a boat.
Hæringr, Þorgrímr's son, was then sixteen years old.
He rode with two men out to Höfði to see Teitr Gizurar-
son. He and Teitr rode, fifteen men strong, to prevent
Helgi from leaving. They met on the Merkrhraun Field
above Mörk near Helgahváll. Helgi had with him two
men who came from Eyrar. Here Helgi and one of his
men fell, and one on Teitr's side. The slain men bal-
anced each other out. (Chap. 10.)

Here the narrative centers upon a verse and a lapidary,
ill-foreboding comment. In such episodes *Landnámabók* is
even more laconic than the sagas. But it is obvious that in
such rough sketches there is contained much of the sagas'
character delineation *in nuce*.[4]

Landnámabók can indeed be regarded as a primitive
form of historical writing. In such a small nation as Iceland the individual persons naturally enough carry more
weight than elsewhere; the history of the country as a whole
and the fate of the individual countrymen are inextricably
entwined.

There were, however, already at an early time Icelandic
scholars who, from the large swarm of individuals, sought
to expose the major lines of development in the nation's
annals and thus to lay the foundation for Icelandic historiography in the actual sense of the word.

Iceland's first historian is Sæmundr inn fróði Sigfússon

(1056–1133).[5] As a young man he studied in Paris and was thus, as far as is known, the first Scandinavian to receive his education there. After his return home he settled down as a priest on his paternal estate at Oddi in the South. In popular tradition Sæmundr has come to appear as somewhat of a sorcerer, a practitioner of white magic. A rich flora of folk tales has also grown up about him, most of which purport that he had gained power over Satan and could force him to perform various services for him.

Sæmundr's work is lost, but with the help of later sources one can draw a number of conclusions about it. Judging from all the evidence, this book was a chronicle which dealt chiefly with the Norwegian kings but simultaneously recorded the most important events in Iceland. It is certain that his work was written in Latin, since Snorri Sturluson states specifically that Ari was the first one to write history in a Scandinavian tongue.

Ari inn fróði Þorgilsson (1067/68–1148), like Sæmundr, was a member of one of Iceland's most respected families. According to the family tree he himself published, he was related by marriage to the Norwegian royal house.

Of Ari's works there is extant a version of *Íslendingabók*, a concise Icelandic history from the earliest settlement times until about 1120.[6] The presentation in this little book—in Hermannsson's edition only twelve pages in length—is concentrated and to the point, without the vivid scenes and lively dialogue of the sagas. Whereas the sagas describe the fate of the individual, Ari is interested first and foremost in chronology, the development of the constitution, and the growth of the church. He determines his chronology with reference to the list of Law Speakers; he indicates how long each Law Speaker held his office.

Ari's only source was oral tradition. But he made use of it with critical acumen; for the sake of certainty he regularly names his informants. Ari praises Þuríðr Snorradóttir as well-informed and reliable in her statements. Since she died in 1113 at the age of eighty-seven, it is obvious that this old woman could have had an essential part of her knowledge directly from people who were born in the tenth century.

As a sample of Ari's description, the section dealing with the colonization of Greenland may be cited:

> The country which is called Greenland was discovered and settled from Iceland.
> Eiríkr rauði was the name of a man from the Breiðafjörður District, who sailed out there and took possession of land at the place which since then has been called Eiríksfjörður. He gave a name to the land and called it Greenland, for he said that people would want to go to that place if the country had a good name. They found there traces of human habitation both in the east and the west of the country and fragments of kayaks and stone implements, from which one can see that the same kind of people had traveled about here who inhabited Vínland and whom the Greenlanders call Skrælings. Eiríkr rauði began to colonize the country fourteen or fifteen years before Christianity came to Iceland, according to what a man who himself accompanied Eiríkr rauði out there told Þorkell Gellisson in Greenland. (Chap. 6.)

Icelandic historiography in the Middle Ages culminated in the work of Snorri Sturluson (1179–1241).[7] We have already met him as one of the leaders in the turbulent political activity in the Sturlung Age. But he made his lasting contribution, as is well known, in the field of literature.

In the monumental work which has since been called *Heimskringla* from the words with which it begins (*Kringla heimsins*, i.e., "The Orb of the World, Orbis terrarum"), Snorri depicts the history of Norway to the time of King Sverrir (1177); the first part of the work, however, *Ynglinga saga*, which is based primarily on the Norwegian poem *Ynglingatal*, deals mostly with the legendary kings of Sweden.[8]

Snorri worked in part with written sources. Among the historical writings in the vernacular which were already in existence in his time is a biography of King Sverrir by the Icelandic abbot Karl Jónsson (d. 1213). In the prologue to his *Heimskringla* Snorri also pays homage to his predecessor Ari for his thorough knowledge of "ancient events, both here and abroad." This prologue also includes a discussion of the value of old skaldic poems as a historical source. Snorri speaks of court poets as early as the time of Haraldr hárfagri:

> With King Haraldr there were skalds, and people still know their poems and poems about all the kings who have since then ruled in Norway. We have the greatest reliance on what is stated in those poems which were recited before the chieftains themselves or their sons. We regard as true everything which these verses relate about their expeditions and battles. It is the custom of skalds to praise him most highly before whom they are standing; yet no one would dare attribute to him deeds which he himself and all within hearing knew to be falsehood and fabrication, for that would be mockery, and not praise.

As a writer of history Snorri thus works more or less like a scientist: he studies the works of his predecessors, collects material from diverse quarters, and exercises a certain critical judgment of his sources. But his striving for historical veracity is accompanied by a delight in the purely artistic shaping of the material. Many episodes from the ancient history of the North—whether they be "historical" or not—have received their classic consummate form in Snorri's powerful and colorful prose. It will suffice to refer here to the dramatic description of the battle at Svoldir. Furthermore, the many added speeches often constitute climaxes in the presentation; an example is the already cited answer of Einarr from Þverá to Óláfr Haraldsson's offer to become the ruler of the Icelanders. In their profuse use of direct speech and dialogue—which, of course, cannot be historical in the strict sense of the word, but is an artistic touch, in their interest in the unique individuality of the characters, and in their plastic form in general, Snorri's sagas of the Norwegian kings closely resemble the most outstanding sagas of Icelanders. According to the greatest expert on Snorri's work in modern times, Snorri's own countryman Sigurður Nordal, he is believed to be the author of *Egils saga* and thus to have had a direct part in the development of the classical saga style.[9]

In any event, Snorri Sturluson was the central figure in the literary activity in Iceland in his day. His name is associated not only with *Heimskringla* but also and especially with the *Edda*. This work is, as the author himself states, designed primarily as a handbook in poetics for young skalds. During the course of the twelfth century the ancient skaldic poetry had got into a critical situation. It had to fight for its existence on two fronts: on the one hand, against the representatives of the church, who looked with misgiving upon all the pagan mythology which is revealed in the kennings, i.e., the form of periphrasis and metaphor peculiar to skaldic language; on the other hand, against the modern simple and easily understood dancing songs, which were considerably more pleasing and caused people to forget the esoteric art of the ancient skalds. One must also admit that skaldic poetry with its uniquely figurative language, its involved word order, and its strict metrical principles could be an intellectual food which was extremely hard to digest.[10] Even the noblemen in whose honor these skaldic verses were so often composed finally grew weary of this austerely inaccessible art and came to prefer lighter forms of literary entertainment.

Snorri's *Edda* consists of four parts: *Prologus, Gylfaginning, Skáldskaparmál, Háttatal.* It is now believed that the last of these was written first. When Snorri returned home from his visit with the Norwegian king, Hákon Hákonarson, and Jarl Skúli in 1220, he composed a poem in honor of both of them which was finished in the winter of 1222/1223. The content of the poem is not very memorable; all the more noteworthy is its form: one hundred and two stanzas in one hundred different meters. The poem, which received the fitting title *Háttatal (List of Meters)*, is thus in itself a sort of practical *ars poetica*. But Snorri interspersed it further with a full metrical commentary in prose.

The art of the skalds, however, consisted not least of all in the manipulation of the specifically poetic words, the so-called *heiti*, and of the kennings. Snorri, therefore, collected numerous examples of these ornaments and arranged them systematically. He illustrated his presentation with authentic ancient skaldic poetry, which to a large degree has been preserved thanks only to his interest. Many of the kennings required a more precise explanation. Why, for example, is skaldic art called by such names as "Suttung's mead," "Kvásir's blood," or "dwarf's drink"? These things cannot be understood without a knowledge of the tales which form the basis of these circumlocutions. And so it came about that Snorri in the *Skáldskaparmál (Poetic Diction)* reproduced a number of old tales about gods, giants, dwarfs, and heroes: about how Óðinn got possession of Suttung's mead, about how the giant women Fenja and Menja ground gold for King Fróði with the mill Grótti, about how Kraki strewed gold over the Fyrisvellir Plains, etc.

Gylfaginning (The Beguiling of Gylfi) presents a comprehensive survey of Old Norse mythology.[11] This section was likewise probably intended originally as an aid to contemporary skaldic art, but for posterity it assumed an entirely different scope and purport. In his *Prologus* Snorri, in accordance with the learned views of the time, had described the Norse gods as actual people, as emigrated descendants of kings of Troy. He supports the story of their origin with a series of curious etymologies. The very designation of the gods (*Áss*; pl., *Æsir*) is thus thought to be derived from the place name *Asia*; *Sif*, the name of Þórr's wife, is the same as *Sibylla*, and so forth. And so in his *Gylfaginning* Snorri has the wise king Gylfi of Sweden betake himself to *Ásgarðr* (the dwelling or world of the *æsir*) in order to ask the gods whence they have received their might. But the *æsir*, who are versed in the art of magic, confound him with optical delusions. Gylfi, who here calls himself Gangleri, is confronted by a pagan trinity, *Hár, Jafnhár,* and *Þriði* ("High," "Equally High," and "The Third"), whom he questions concerning the world's origin, the gods, and the destruction of the world. Snorri has them relate such classic tales as the one about Þórr's journey to Útgarða-Loki, or the story of Baldr's death. In the end Gylfi is freed from the enchantment:

> Thereupon Gangleri heard loud noises from every direction and he glanced to one side. And when he had looked about him more, he found he was standing out on a level field, and he didn't see hall or castle any longer. Then he went on his way and came home to his kingdom and told about the things he had seen and heard. And all the people told these tales to each other just as he had told them.
>
> But the *æsir* sat down to talk and to take counsel, and they recalled all the tales they had told him. And they gave the same names that were already used to the men and places there so that, after a long time had passed, people should not doubt that those *æsir* who were just spoken of and these who were given the same names were all one and the same.

Those old pagan myths are presented by Snorri as a delusion, as a conjuration perpetrated by unscrupulous illusionists for the purpose of arrogating to themselves divine power and worship. The author of *Gylfaginning* was, after all, a Christian himself; in the frame-narrative as well as in the prologue he expresses the opinion that the *æsir* religion was a heathen deception. Scholars in the field of the history of religion must, therefore, use Snorri's work with discretion. One must not forget that Iceland had been Christian for over two hundred years when he undertook to collect and present the ancient mythology. But in spite of sources of error which are difficult to determine, his work is indispensable for our knowledge of the pagan beliefs of the North. Just as Snorri illustrated the use of kennings with various quotations from authentic skaldic poetry, he supported his portrayal of the mythology with a great many stanzas from ancient poems such as *Völuspá*. It is certain that Snorri himself took part in the collection of the poems which today are known as the *Poetic Edda*.[12]

Snorri's *Edda* was, as has been said, intended primarily as a book of instruction for skalds. And, as a matter of fact, skaldic poetry did experience a renaissance during the thirteenth century. But this work has not been without influence on saga literature also. The many interspersed skaldic verses, such as we find in *Skáldskaparmál*, are also characteristic of the Sagas of Icelanders. Occasionally, when the central figure is a skald, the verses seem to have comprised the nucleus around which the story was constructed. Sometimes they serve as a sort of verification of the truthfulness of the content of the story. The writers of later sagas hit upon the idea of putting fabricated, "ungenuine" verses in the mouths of the saga characters. Snorri's work must, therefore, have stimulated interest in and knowledge of the tremendous number of *lausavísur*, i.e., individual occasional verses connected with a definite situation or episode.

The learned men of Iceland, however, did not devote themselves exclusively to the writing of history and to related branches of investigation. During the first half of the twelfth century a zealous effort was made to find a system of writing suitable for the Icelandic language. An anonymous scholar wrote a study on the subject which is generally called the *First Grammatical Treatise*.[13] The author reveals an unusually keen power of observation, and he succeeded in creating a system which satisfies the highest demands. He seems to have received his education in England and France, and he proves to be well-versed in Latin. Therefore it is all the more remarkable that he did not shrink back from writing his difficult theoretical linguistic analysis in his mother tongue. This is an excellent example of the independence with which the Icelandic bearers of culture at that time could adopt and adapt the learning common to Europe.

Nor did Icelandic interest in study and authorship restrict itself to the purely humanistic area. There are treatises in Icelandic on mathematics, astronomy, and the establishment of the calendar. In the oldest of these, dating from the twelfth century, there are contained among other things some observations on the course of the sun which are attributed to a person called Stjörnu-Oddi ("Star-Oddi"). Later scientists have shown that Oddi, although he scarcely could have had instruments of any kind, made remarkably exact observations without falling into errors which at that time were common in other parts of the world.

The Icelandic sagas about native heroes were thus written during a period of richly diversified literary activity in the twelfth and thirteenth centuries. As a genre these sagas were not at all isolated. They bordered more or less on other forms of prose narrative writing which are also designated with the term *saga*. The Sagas of Kings have already been mentioned. They dealt with kings and other nobles, primarily those of Norway, but also with the earls of the Orkneys, chieftains of the Faroe Islands, and Danish kings. With Snorri Sturluson's *Heimskringla* this kind of historical writing reached its culmination. The designation contemporary sagas, or sagas of contemporary times, has been given to biographies of spiritual and secular leaders in Iceland during the literary period. They were written for the most part by men who themselves knew these leaders and took part in the events depicted or at least had access to eyewitnesses. The compilation *Sturlunga*, which was used above to characterize Icelandic conditions in the thirteenth century, is also a contemporary saga. To this genre belong further a series of biographies of the native bishops. These are often strongly colored by the international ecclesiastical literature of the time.

If the Sagas of Kings and the sagas of contemporary times are historical in principle, the opposite is the case with the so-called *fornaldarsögur*, or sagas of ancient times.[14] The action in these stories takes place before the time of Haraldr hárfagri and the colonization of Iceland, in a period which precedes that of the Sagas of Icelanders. They always take place outside of Iceland and make no claim to historical correctness. Even if certain traits can be regarded as authentic, we are dealing here in general with fiction written for the purpose of entertaining. *Fornaldarsögur* existed in oral form as early as the twelfth century; but it is thought that they were not written down before the thirteenth century, especially during the latter decades, when the other, more native and more highly regarded saga literature began to decline.

Just where the Sagas of Icelanders are to be located on the line which is bounded by the extreme points history and pure fiction, i.e., whether from this special point of view they stand closer to a work such as *Sturlunga* or to the *fornaldarsögur*, is a controversial problem which is difficult to solve. This problem is closely related to the question of the relative importance of oral tradition and literary authorship in the Sagas of Icelanders, which is a question of such general and fundamental interest that it will be discussed separately in the next chapter.

This extraordinarily powerful literary development in Iceland during the Middle Ages has often been characterized as some sort of miracle. This memorable achievement was made by a nation which scarcely numbered more than sixty to seventy thousand persons, who on the whole must have lived in meager external circumstances. The literary genius of these Icelanders, the quality of their work, can of course never be satisfactorily explained. It will always remain a "wonder." But the matter also has quantitative, more easily measurable aspects, as Sigurður Nordal recently set forth in an interesting essay.[15]

The writing and copying of manuscripts must have been a very widespread activity in Iceland, not only to record original works but above all to make copies of them. Some of the better known and more popular works must have reached relatively large "editions." Thus there are still extant twenty-one vellum manuscripts of *Njáls saga* and thirteen of *Egils saga Skalla-Grímssonar*. According to the estimate of experts there now remain about seven hundred skin manuscripts written by Icelanders before the middle of the sixteenth century. But many of them are merely fragments, sometimes consisting of a single leaf; on the whole, it is extremely rare to meet with a complete codex. From all indications old manuscripts in large number must have been lost in the course of the centuries. How many can never be known. But judging from certain signs, those we still have must represent far less than one-tenth of the original manuscript material.

All these manuscripts required a great deal of parchment. For the famous *Flateyjarbók*, which was written between 1380 and 1390 and comprises almost four hundred folio pages, one hundred calves, according to Nordal, had to lose their skins. There is really good reason to ask how a relatively poor nation of farmers could afford the luxury of using so much leather for "unproductive" intellectual matters. But agriculture in Iceland during the Middle Ages was based entirely on the raising of livestock, and the number of cattle on the large farms was considerable. And yet, it would scarcely have been possible to afford the use of calfskin on such a large scale for parchment if it had not been for the fact that the hides which were best suited for precisely that purpose—those of suckling calves—were practically worthless for any other use. But also the work required for preparing the parchment was an important economic factor. How was it possible for the Icelanders to occupy themselves with such a production of luxuries? To a certain degree this also was based on the Icelandic type of farming. There was no sowing, for the Icelandic farmers seldom cultivated grain; as a consequence, they were also spared the work of harvesting and threshing in the fall. The winter season was long and could provide much free time, at least for the men.

If the Icelanders had had to depend on the importation of expensive parchment, many manuscripts would certainly have remained unwritten. Their own unique supplies of calfskin and time, in a fortunate manner, favored their literary activity.

Oral Tradition and Literary Authorship, History and Fiction in the Sagas of Icelanders

THERE IS GENERAL AGREEMENT among scholars that most of the Sagas of Icelanders were written in the thirteenth century. But the content of this extensive literature was Icelandic life during the so-called Saga Age—the century from 930, when the General Assembly was established and the new state could be regarded as constituted, until 1030, when Christianity had been the official religion in Iceland for a period of one generation. Does the writing of the sagas in the thirteenth century signify merely the definitive fixation of an essentially historical tradition, which for two or three hundred years, generation after generation, had faithfully preserved the memory of people and events in the Saga Age? Or is it a question of pure fiction, the creation of the authors' imaginative speculations about the past, possibly supported by certain historical data, especially such as was found in genealogical lists and similar records from the twelfth century?

Independent of, but closely related to, this pair of alternatives is another dichotomy: that between oral narrative art and individual literary authorship. If the sagas as we know them from the manuscripts were already completely formed in oral tradition—as the so-called free-prose theory maintains—one would not have the right to speak of the writers as authors; their role would be merely that of a clerk or recorder. If, on the other hand, the sagas are primarily the products of individual authors—as the so-called book-prose theory asserts—they must be regarded as the

49

creation of a powerful literary movement in Iceland during the thirteenth century.

These two problems, as has been observed, go hand in hand. The scholars who consider the Sagas of Icelanders to be more or less historical naturally like to believe in the definitive significance of oral tradition in their literary shaping as well. Those who have a low estimate of the historical veracity of these sagas are, on the other hand, more inclined to see them as works of individual authors.

It is understandable that the study of the Icelandic sagas should have been strongly concentrated on these two questions. Their solution is not only important for an evaluation of the sagas as a literary genre, as epic art; it is also conclusive in regard to the value one can attribute to this literature as a source of information in the areas of older Scandinavian customs, ethics, and religion.

The clash of opinions among scholars has been sharp. Thus, weighty blows were exchanged in 1910 between two Icelanders, Björn Magnússon Ólsen and Finnur Jónsson, in a learned duel about *Gunnlaugs saga ormstungu*.[1] The former had tried to prove in a treatise that this saga was the work of a well-read author who had made copious use of other previously written sagas. Finnur Jónsson, in accordance with his general view of saga literature, namely, that the chief source was oral tradition of great historical reliability, rejected his countryman's thesis.

Actually, those who hold to the sagas' historical authenticity and their close dependence on a strong oral tradition are from the outset at a certain disadvantage in this controversy. The possibilities of checking the sagas' statements with the help of other sources are very limited. And for obvious reasons it is impossible to demonstrate what these sagas were like in their alleged oral stage. All things considered, the only evidence we have to go by are the preserved manuscripts, the written saga literature. On the other hand, even a superficial study makes it clear that the sagas cannot possibly be pure fiction without any trace of history or oral tradition behind them. It is absurd to regard (as a Danish literary historian has actually done) even the detailed family trees "which, indeed, are among the sagas' most important embellishments" as a completely fabricated element.[2] Since various sagas deal with the same persons, one would in that case have to assume that a group of novel writers had agreed to use a common gallery of characters and that they had carried out this fabrication with unfaltering consistency— a daring hypothesis indeed!

The most thoroughly methodical attempt to portray the Icelandic sagas as the product of a long oral tradition preserved by uncommonly good memory was made by the Norwegian Knut Liestøl in his book *Upphavet til den islendske ættesaga* (1929).[3] He regards the sagas written in Iceland as the final phase of a richly developed oral narrative art which had deep roots in the home districts of the Norwegian emigrants. To be sure, Liestøl is forced to admit that medieval Norway itself completely lacks family traditions of the type reflected in the Icelandic sagas. He reminds us, however, that precisely those districts of Norway from which the original settlers chiefly came have always been especially distinguished for their wealth of poetry and tales. The art of the Icelandic sagas is thus said to have a strong foundation in the Norwegian motherland.

For people nowadays it must certainly seem odd that narratives which fill several hundred printed pages should have been memorized and transmitted practically verbatim from one generation to the next. But in former times, when the art of writing was unknown or at best known to very few, conditions must have been far more favorable for oral tradition than in our day. A person was simply compelled to store in his memory all sorts of facts and figures which one today can look up in books. The Icelandic Law Speaker, for example, was originally supposed to recite the entire body of law at the General Assembly during his three-year period of office. The very purpose and intention of remembering something must formerly have strengthened memory and recollection in a manner different from today, when there are so many possibilities of relieving one's memory. It also seems reasonable that the concentration required for memorization could have been much greater in an older, more primitive and more homogeneous society than in our modern, complicated culture with its tremendous and continuous piling up of new material through books, newspapers, radio, movies, television, etc.

But in the old Icelandic community there may perhaps have existed other special conditions favoring a reliable oral tradition. One often senses in the sagas a remarkable concern that certain deeds should really be remembered and reported. An episode in *Egils saga* describes how Kveld-Úlfr and his son Skalla-Grímr with their followers "clear" one of the king's ships which they come upon. They kill all men on board except two or three, the ones they regard as least important. In return these have to tell what men were on board and what their errand was. Then they are released and ordered to betake themselves to the king and to report accurately to him what had happened and which opponents of his had carried out the deed. The thought of renown after death can for the characters in the sagas be a powerful incentive to do their utmost, not least of all in hopeless situations. They fight without compromise, boldly defy fate, in order that their last hours at least may be worth telling about. They already see themselves, so to speak, in the light of history.

It is clear that the Icelanders at an early date gained a reputation for having good memories and for being reliable in their statements about the past. It is scarcely a coincidence that they practically acquired a monopoly over the office of court skald for the Norwegian kings. In this position they functioned practically as royal historiographers who in their poems drew the picture of the rulers' military deeds; it will be remembered that Snorri in his kings' sagas attached great importance to the testimony of the skalds.

A young Icelander in the retinue of Haraldr harðráði according to his own biography related to the king himself the history of the latter's expeditions abroad.[4] Haraldr was greatly impressed by the fact that the extensive report was correct in every detail. But the Icelander declared he had acquired this knowledge at home at the General Assembly from a countryman who had accompanied the king. It was at the General Assembly that the Icelanders had a center of unexampled significance for the exchange of news. Here every summer people from all parts of the country came together. For most of them the journey to and from Þingvellir took several days, and there could be quite a few persons traveling together. In every district they came to on the way, new views opened up over places that were well known in tradition. Even the treeless and massively rugged landscape, the broad vistas as such, must have facilitated the synthesis. The scene of action for an entire saga or for several sagas could open up before the travelers. This helped the imagination create a unity in the happenings. Some of the most memorable deeds of the past had occurred right at Þingvellir. Here many threads of tradition were drawn together. Both the journeys to and fro as well as the stay at the Assembly itself provided ample opportunity for *sagnaskemmtan*—the Icelandic term for the pastime of telling stories about actual or fictitious events. Among the more highly regarded kinds of entertainment of this kind were certainly reports by men who had traveled abroad about their more or less noteworthy experiences; we sometimes read that such men attracted listeners especially at the Assembly. Such episodes were scarcely unusual. The Icelanders of the Commonwealth seem, in general, to have been an active people. Voyages abroad were common. But one also receives a strong impression of active communication within the country itself. Testimony for the lively connection among various parts of the country in both ancient and modern times is found, for example, in the fact that the language, practically speaking, completely lacks dialectal cleavage.

Travel and active social intercourse, together with a firm mooring in an isolated and sparsely populated land, are factors which could have favored the rise and spread of chronicles of families or districts. But one must also consider the structure of the small Icelandic state itself. In larger countries with a strong central government the individual was pushed into an out-of-the-way corner by the masses or by more impersonal and abstract factors. But in Iceland with its lack of a national government and an executive power one scarcely perceived the group for the individuals. In this society, which has been called an aristo-democracy, each yeoman farmer sat like a little king over his ofttimes extensive landholdings. The history of such individuals was also the history of Iceland. This must have intensified the individual's feeling of self-esteem and his interest in what tradition had to say about his own family's achievements.

Here some of the reasons have been cited which are usually referred to in support of the view that the Icelandic sagas of native heroes really *could* have had a reliable oral tradition of several hundred years behind them. But such reflections, of course, do not constitute positive proof. Liestøl, however, collected from the written sagas a number of characteristic features of style, composition, theme, and character delineation which he regarded as evidence that these narratives had previously had a long existence in oral form. From his analysis he drew the conclusion that not only the content of a saga but also its linguistic form could have been fixed during the oral period and that this oral form could have been transmitted to the parchment practically verbatim. Liestøl's argumentation largely revolves

54

around general considerations and sometimes betrays the fact that the assumptions with which he begins are actually what he is trying to prove.

A feature of the Icelandic sagas which is very striking is their unique style. When the same or similar situations recur, the same turn of phrase is often resorted to. "Þorsteinn was the name of a man"—with this expression many a saga begins, and it is regularly used to introduce a new character. If the action shifts or if the saga takes up a new thread, this is indicated by some such set phrase as "Now it must be told about Þorgeirr Otkelsson." Furthermore, it is not only the most common situations which are introduced with such conventional words, but also others which do not recur so frequently. All this is considered by Liestøl to be a natural result of oral transmission. In writing one strives for variety of expression. The oral tale, on the other hand, has a tendency to use the same words when it describes the same or similar actions. The ofttimes similar themes of the sagas influence each other even in phraseology. This is a principle which holds true for all old forms of oral tradition. The ballad, the folk tale, and the legend all have their distinctive, fixed, and somewhat monotonous style, with standing formulas for identical or similar situations.

But the uniqueness of saga style is said to depend not only on the circumstance that several tales of the same kind live in the memory of the individual saga-teller and color each other there. According to Liestøl this uniqueness also results from the fact that one man after another relates the same story. The series of sagamen, so to speak, cancel out each other's peculiarities; the individual stamp which the recitation of each one can have had is rubbed off during the course of tradition and transmission. There evolves a homogeneous, harmonious form of style which everyone becomes accustomed to and which is regarded as normal and suitable for this kind of tale—partly because this style came into being in the mouths of the people. Liestøl goes so far as to attribute, at least in part, even the famous objectivity of the Icelandic sagas to this strongly sloughed-off style, which gives expression to an impersonal or collective mode of thought.

There are also other characteristics of saga style which, according to Liestøl, can be derived from their oral preservation and presentation. He is not thinking here primarily of the lucid construction of sentences consisting of co-ordinate clauses in place of the more highly involved periods with inserted subordinate clauses, the natural word order, and the rhythm in general, which is most effective when the sagas are read aloud. A literary author can also strive to achieve this kind of style. But much of what strikes us as uneven and disjointed in the language of the sagas can, according to Liestøl, be explained most simply as the result of an oral manner of expression. The saga not seldom breaks off one construction and continues with another without regard for the demands of logic (anacoluthon). Direct and indirect quotation can alternate unexpectedly with each other, and the tense of narration changes back and forth with no apparent reason between present and imperfect, not seldom within one and the same sentence.[5] Such irregularities in writing have a distracting effect, but an animated oral presentation clears up their meaning immediately.

The characteristics of saga style, however, which Liestøl interprets as criteria of a long oral tradition are not convincing. They do not preclude the possibility that the sagas are purely the product of individual authors. For when one first begins to make use of the vernacular for prose fiction, it is after all quite plausible that this prose should reveal a number of features typical of colloquial speech. In such a situation the spoken language is almost the only native model one has to go by.

In order to elucidate how oral tradition gradually models historical material, Liestøl made a comparison between the Sagas of Icelanders on the one hand and *Sturlunga* on the other. The latter, like the sagas of native heroes, was written during the thirteenth century, but it does not depict events which occurred two to three hundred years before; instead, it gives a broad chronicle of Icelandic history during the twelfth and thirteenth centuries. According to Liestøl, it is clear that *Sturlunga* also strove to attain the classic saga style. But at the same time, he maintained, it is significant that this work, because of the immediacy of the material, became chaotically rich in details and, therefore, completely lacks the unification, the composition, and the artistic formation in general which characterize the classical sagas as a whole. *Sturlunga* is said to show the historical tradition in a raw condition, as it appears before the so-called epic laws have had time to exert their influence. This difference—it was previously described eloquently and humorously by Hans E. Kinck[6]—is finely and correctly observed, but the inference which Liestøl draws from it is too hasty. The dissimilarity cannot simply be interpreted as a confirmation of the refining effect of oral tradition. As a matter of fact, the features of style and composition characteristic of the sagas are not limited to oral tales about authentic persons and events which in the course of time were formed in accordance with certain artistic rules. If a given saga were the work of a creative, imaginative author, its contents would have been formed and molded along similar lines.

On the other hand, it must be admitted that the sagas sometimes are encumbered with things that look more like remnants of a historical tradition than the contribution of a creative author. Thus, for example, there are series of names and individual episodes that for the modern reader's taste, at least, take up too much space and overload the story. They do not give evidence of a well-executed artistic economy in the usual sense, but can be thought of as a surviving reminiscence of the variegated wealth of material of life itself. Even if this be the case, one still does not know how great the significance of the historical element is for the saga as a whole or how firm a form it had in oral tradition.

Similar objections can be directed against other arguments of the free-prose theory. It has been pointed out, for example, that the sagas themselves time after time state that news of happenings was heard quickly and far about, or that someone related a noteworthy event he had witnessed to a large circle of listeners, or that some person was questioned in great detail about what had happened on a certain occasion. Some scholars have tried to interpret such statements as an indication that the sagas began to assume their form almost simultaneously with the happenings they describe. But people have always talked and will continue to talk in this way about their experiences without ever having any "sagas" grow from these seeds. In the sagas one frequently comes upon such statements as "people say," "it is reported," "according to what most people say," and the like; according to Liestøl such references are a direct indication of oral tradition. Actually, it is likely that such formulations in time became a mannerism, a trait of narrative technique. But the fact that they occur so profusely was regarded as an indication that they must have deep roots in the past. Here too, however, the objection arises that one cannot gain the slightest concept of how large a part this oral tradition could have had in the content and form of the written sagas.

As is well known, dialogue plays an extraordinarily large role in the Sagas of Icelanders, so large that the story for long stretches can take on a purely dramatic character. With the support of other oral tradition Liestøl asserts that the dialogue could have occurred in the contemporary descriptions of historical events. He admits, however, that not a few of the conversations must have been fabricated. Thus, for example, secret conversations between two persons are sometimes related; in reality, of course, no one could have found out what was said on such an occasion. Sometimes repartee is used to inform a person quite unnecessarily about matters which are already well known to both speakers; actually, of course, dialogue of such a nature is created to inform the listener or reader—an artistic expedient well known, for example, from the French classical drama. But the question is whether the dialogues in the sagas should not in principle be judged as fiction. In the longer sagas conversations among various persons take place in endless combinations at various places and at different times; often, as already mentioned, secret discussions occur between only two persons. If the dialogues of such sagas were authentic, this would have to imply in any case that a reporter had access to statements from a large number of eyewitnesses or from one of the participants and, in addition, possessed the necessary view of the whole so as to work these statements into a large and often complicated context. This scarcely sounds plausible.

But even if we regard conversation in the sagas essentially as fiction, one has still not taken a position in regard to the question of whether this fiction belongs to oral tradition or only to the written saga. Liestøl believes that the art of dialogue must have developed during oral transmission, and that it was this life on the tongues of the people from generation to generation which gave the repartee its pithy terseness. As an example of a concise and well-constructed dialogue he cites a short conversation from *Ljósvetninga saga*. The chieftain Guðmundr inn ríki, a man who reveals the bearing of a bully combined with personal cowardice, meets Ófeigr at a certain farm. Guðmundr is assigned the seat of honor, and Ófeigr, the place next to him.

> When the tables were brought, Ófeigr laid his fist on the table and said, "Don't you think this fist is large, Guðmundr?"
> He answered, "Large it is."

59

Ófeigr said, "Do you believe there's any strength in it?"

Guðmundr said, "I certainly do."

Ófeigr said, "Do you believe it can deliver a hard blow?"

Guðmundr said, "Terribly hard."

Ófeigr said, "What kind of damage do you think would come of it?"

Guðmundr said, "Broken bones or death."

Ófeigr said, "How do you think death like that would be?"

Guðmundr said, "Very bad. I wouldn't want to die like that.

Ófeigr said, "Then don't sit in my place."

Guðmundr said, "Just as you say." And he sat down on the other side of the table. (Chap. 11.)

Probably many persons, in opposition to Liestøl, would see in such a finely chiseled dialogue the result of a pronounced literary conventionalization.

The extant manuscripts of Icelandic sagas are practically never originals; they are copies, often with a long series of predecessors. The individual scribes in those days seldom showed exaggerated piety for the wording of the anonymous works they copied. Various transcripts of the text of one and the same saga could, therefore, gradually come to deviate more or less from each other. To the extent that one has access to such variants one can through a meticulous analysis and comparison of the texts attempt to determine the relationship between them or, under the most favorable conditions, reconstruct a reasonably close approximation of the original. Some scholars, however, insist that certain deviations between two manuscripts are of such a kind that they cannot come from a scribe but must go back to different oral versions which were recorded independently of each other. If one could identify such cases with certainty, they would naturally constitute a valuable support for the free-prose theory. In order to give a more definite concept of the problem and the argumentation, we shall discuss here one example from Liestøl's book. It is not a matter of two variants of the same saga, but rather the treatment in two different sagas of one and the same episode. The problem in principle, however, is exactly the same.

Gísli Súrsson, the chief person in one of the longer sagas, had been slain. The most prominent man connected with his killing, which was accomplished with vastly superior numbers, was named Eyjólfr. Gísli's sister Þórdís was at that time married to Börkr, the brother of Þorgrímr, who had been slain by Gísli. Thus the relationship among the characters is complicated: Gísli is the blood brother of Þórdís, but at the same time the killer of her first husband; he is the brother-in-law of Börkr, but also the slayer of his brother. (When Börkr married Þórdís, he did not yet know that his future brother-in-law had killed his brother.) The episode which describes how Eyjólfr, the leader of the men who killed Gísli, visited Börkr inn digri and Þórdís and related what had happened is found both in *Gísla saga Súrssonar* itself and in *Eyrbyggja saga*. In the former the text is as follows:

> Now Eyjólfr set out from his place with eleven men and went southward to visit Börkr inn digri, and he told him all the details of what had happened. Börkr became merry at this, and he asked Þórdís to give him a hearty welcome—"and remember the great love you had for my brother Þorgrímr, and treat Eyjólfr well."
>
> "I shall grieve for my brother Gísli," said Þórdís. "But will Gísli's killer not have hospitality enough if I cook and give him some porridge?"
>
> In the evening, when she served the food, she dropped the tray of spoons. Eyjólfr had laid the sword which had belonged to Gísli under the table near his feet. Þórdís recognized the sword, and when she bent down for the spoons, she seized the hilt of the sword and thrust it up at Eyjólfr. She wanted to strike him in the middle

61

of his body, but she did not notice that the guard was turned up, and it caught under the table. The blow landed lower than she had intended; it struck the thigh and inflicted a great wound. Börkr seized Þórdís and wrenched the sword from her hands. They all jumped up and thrust back the tables with the food. Börkr offered to let Eyjólfr determine his own compensation for the wound, and Eyjólfr awarded himself full wergild, declaring he would have demanded more if Börkr had not acted so well.

Thereupon Þórdís named witnesses and announced her separation from Börkr. She declared she would never again share the same bed with him, and she never did. (Chap. 37.)

In the version of the same episode found in *Eyrbyggja saga* an additional person plays a prominent part, namely, the fourteen-year-old Snorri, son of Þórdís and her first husband, Þorgrímr. Börkr is thus Snorri's uncle and stepfather. When the death of Gísli was reported, we read in *Eyrbyggja* that

Börkr grew very gleeful, and he called upon Þórdís and Snorri to welcome Eyjólfr warmly, since he had removed such a great disgrace from them and their kinsmen. Snorri appeared not to be moved much by this news, but Þórdís said it would be a good enough welcome—"if porridge were given the killer of Gísli."

Börkr retorted, "I don't care what kind of food you prepare."

Börkr had Eyjólfr sit in the seat of honor and placed his followers on both sides of him. They laid their weapons on the floor. Börkr sat next to Eyjólfr, and Snorri beside Börkr. Þórdís brought in the porridge bowls to the table, and she was also holding the spoons. While she was placing a bowl before Eyjólfr, she dropped one of the spoons. Stooping down for it, she seized Eyjólfr's sword, drew it quickly, and thrust it up under the table into his thigh. The guard caught on the table, and yet it was a great wound.

Börkr thrust the table away and struck Þórdís. Snorri shoved Börkr so hard that he fell. He put his arm around his mother and said she had been tormented enough, as it was, without being beaten. Eyjólfr and his followers jumped up, but Börkr's men held them back. The outcome of the matter was that Börkr gave Eyjólfr the right to determine the indemnity himself and paid him a large sum of money for the injury. Thereupon Eyjólfr rode away. Because of this affair the ill will between Börkr and Snorri increased greatly. (Chap. 13.)

In both sagas the episode is of about equal length, and the content also is essentially the same. But Liestøl concentrates on the points of difference: in *Gísla saga* Þórdís lets a tray of spoons fall, but in *Eyrbyggja* she drops only one spoon; in *Gísla saga* Börkr seizes Þórdís and takes the sword away from her, while in *Eyrbyggja* he tries to strike her and is himself knocked down by Snorri, etc. These differences, declares Liestøl, must indicate oral variants. He obviously believes that such differences in detail—a spoon instead of a tray of spoons, for example—would scarcely result from the adaptation of a written source. The very fact that they are incidental details with no significance for the action would prevent them from being deliberately omitted or changed. But it is difficult to see why it is necessary to come to such a conclusion. One need not assume that a writer had his written source before him at the time he was working on it. He may have read it, or heard it read, at some time in the past, and he now recollects its essential content along with some of its phraseology. He can deal quite freely with details without thereby distorting the picture as a whole.

The most obvious and most important difference in the two versions of this episode is the fact that *Eyrbyggja* introduces Snorri and assigns to him a very active role. As a sort of end result of the scene, it is also stated specifically that this increased the ill will between Snorri and his stepfather Börkr. Projecting Snorri into the foreground in this way is altogether natural and fitting in *Eyrbyggja*, since he occupies such a prominent place in that saga from this chapter on. It is evident that the episode was shaped with regard to the particular purpose of this saga. In *Gísla saga*, on the other hand, there is no reason to concentrate attention on Snorri; there, interest is centered exclusively on Þórdís' reaction to the news of the slaying of her brother. There appears to be nothing to prevent one from assuming that one saga borrowed the episode from the other, or that each saga independently borrowed it from a common written source and adapted it to its own particular needs. On the other hand, it is admittedly conceivable that each of the two textual variants actually derives from its own oral version. But so far as one can see, Liestøl has not succeeded in proving or even in making it seem plausible that this is the case. The same objection applies to his other alleged examples of oral variants.

The present-day tendency in saga research certainly runs diametrically counter to the free-prose theory as represented by Liestøl. This is true, in any case, of what one could call the Icelandic school of scholars with Sigurður Nordal as leader. Nordal's short treatise *Hrafnkatla* (1940) is a milestone;[7] the title of this work was created by the author as a designation for *Hrafnkels saga* by analogy to such Icelandic forms as *Njála*, *Eigla*, *Grettla*, etc. This masterpiece of the saga genre is, to be sure, very well known; but in the interest of clarity a condensed summary of the short saga will be given here before Nordal's argumentation is discussed.

The powerful chieftain and godi Hrafnkell was a zealous worshiper of Freyr and, therefore, acquired the cognomen Freysgoði. With Freyr he shared equally his most precious possessions, including a magnificent stallion which he called Freyfaxi. Hrafnkell had sworn a solemn oath that he would be the death of any man who rode this stallion against his will. His sheep herdsman, a young man by the name of Einarr, once transgressed against this prohibition, and Hrafnkell slew him. Einarr's cousin Sámr brought suit against Hrafnkell for manslaughter at the General Assembly, even though the undertaking seemed to be hopeless. Just when he was on the point of giving up, he received unexpected help from two brothers, Þorkell and Þorgeirr Þjóstarsson, who had come from the western districts with a large body of followers. Hrafnkell was sentenced to outlawry and was driven away from his estate, Aðalból, where Sámr now made his abode. The pagan temple on the farm was burned down and Freyfaxi was killed by being pushed off a cliff. Hrafnkell settled down in a neighboring district, where he soon prospered again and once more became a powerful man. Finally the time was ripe for retaliation. Hrafnkell killed Sámr's brother Eyvindr and chased Sámr himself away from Aðalból. Thereafter Hrafnkell remained as a respected man on his old estate as long as he lived.

Nordal points out the fact that *Hrafnkatla* quite generally has been regarded as one of the historically most reliable sagas of native heroes. Consequently people thought that it had been changed very little by the saga writer; it had existed, so they believed, in practically finished form in oral tradition. It is also difficult to find any points at which to attack the historical reliability of *Hrafnkatla,* since there are few sources with which to compare it. The description is free of suspicious exaggerations, it lacks the conventional boasting about great deeds performed by Icelanders abroad, and it shows no noticeable influence of either foreign literature or other Icelandic sagas.[8] *Hrafnkatla* is an exceptionally consistent and well-rounded work. All doubt about its veracity seems doomed to bounce off it without effect.

First of all, Nordal subjected the two sons of Þjóstarr from the West Fjords to close examination. These two men suddenly turn up at the General Assembly as helpers just

65

when Sámr and his uncle Þorbjörn find all roads to success in their case blocked. They play a decisive role in the story, for it is they who bring about the dramatic turn in the course of events. They are absolutely indispensable. But these brothers, Þorkell and Þorgeirr, are mentioned nowhere else than in *Hrafnkatla*. *Landnámabók*, on the other hand, mentions their father Þjóstarr and their brother Þormóðr. One wonders why such a document should preserve the memory of Þormóðr but fail to mention his brothers Þorkell and Þorgeirr, who, judging from *Hrafnkatla*, must have been much more powerful than he. The silence surrounding them is indeed surprising. The action of a number of sagas takes place in and around the Vestfirðir or in the Breiðafjörður District during the tenth century. In view of the influence and the temperament of the sons of Þjóstarr, as they are portrayed in *Hrafnkatla*, one should expect that they would have taken an active part in the affairs depicted in these sagas. But there is no mention anywhere either of the two men themselves or of their descendants. "A remarkable thing seems to have happened in the case of these chieftains from the West Fjords," says Nordal, "for their memory has been preserved nowhere else than in a saga from a distant region of the country." The story takes place in northeastern Iceland. On top of all this, a comparison with other sources shows that there was no room for the sons of Þjóstarr to live as chieftains in the district designated by the saga, for all the land there was already occupied by persons with a better right to be regarded as historical than theirs. Everything that is said in *Hrafnkatla* about their influence and exploits must be pure fabrication. But the rapid rise of Hrafnkell Freysgoði to power and prestige in his new home after his defeat has also been proven to be historically impossible; for, according to *Landnámabók*, a certain Brynjólfr gamli and his family held sway over this region. Therefore, there was no more room for Hrafnkell to exercise authority in this district than there was for the sons of Þjóstarr in the Þorskafjörður.

Thus in a number of crucial points the supporting framework of the action of *Hrafnkatla* has been proven to be fictitious, and consequently the belief in the historical reliability of this saga collapses. Nordal devotes two fascinating chapters of his study to an analysis of *Hrafnkatla* as a work of art—to its composition, style, and character portrayal. He finds here an artistic creation which far surpasses everything which one is accustomed to associate with the more primitive art of oral narration. *Hrafnkatla* is a literary epic on such a high level of development that it "deceives the reader and impresses him as being a perfect example of orally-transmitted narrative such as he imagines oral narration ought to have been." The results of Nordal's investigation can be suitably summarized by his own words: "Thus it seems altogether reasonable and even necessary to regard *Hrafnkatla* as the work of one author, whose intention was not to relate a true story, but to compose a work of fiction—as the work of a man who was endowed with a vivid imagination, a knowledge of human nature, and poetic boldness and who was carried to such heights by one of the most powerful literary movements in history." (p. 68.)

Admittedly the question of history versus fiction, oral tradition versus individual authorship has not been answered once and for all by Nordal's contribution. He himself has demanded emphatically that each saga must be examined individually with regard to its historical veracity, its sources, and its treatment of subject matter. But when *Hrafnkatla*, regarded as among the historically most reliable sagas, is exposed as a work of fiction, one must be on guard against alleged historical tradition in other cases, too.[9]

In spite of the undeniable homogeneity of this literary genre, the sagas of native heroes upon closer inspection reveal significant differences as well as a definite chronological development. Thanks primarily to Nordal, this development of saga writing and of saga style can now be seen in a new light. Nordal criticizes the intransigent belief of certain older scholars that the best sagas must also have been the oldest, and that an inferior style and defective composition were indications of a later date of origin. He replaces this picture of an early classical age followed by progressive decay with a development curve which seems intrinsically to be more plausible. He envisions the beginning of saga writing as groping and feeling its way. Saga style gradually acquires its typical character through a synthesis of two widely differing stylistic elements. On the one hand, there was the relatively primitive technique of oral narration, with its abrupt and frequently awkward diction, somewhat as if the narrator were short of breath. On the other hand, there was the foreign ecclesiastical style as found in numerous translations, which is broad, complicated, and verbose. Nordal characterizes the fusion of these two elements of style as follows: "The Icelanders succeeded—thanks both to their knowledge of the Latin literary language and translations of it from about 1100 on—in creating for themselves a saga style from these two contrasts, and in uniting much of the simplicity of colloquial speech with the richness of the language of books." In some of the older sagas it is possible, according to Nordal, to observe how the author laboriously struggles with the task of combining the two opposites into a unified style. In the second half of the thirteenth century a better balance between the different stylistic elements is achieved: one is approaching the classical saga style.

Detailed comparisons between manuscript variants of one and the same saga appear definitely to corroborate this survey of the development as a whole. It was plausibly demonstrated, for instance, that a more "classical" manuscript of *Fóstbrœðra saga* represents a later polished edition of an older, peculiar version with certain baroque stylistic embellishments of a learned, poetic, or religious nature.

(See page 16 above.) According to Nordal, Snorri Sturluson, who wrote his sagas of kings from diverse older sources with varying styles, played a decisive role in this process of equalization. If, as Nordal and others have convincingly maintained, Snorri was actually the author of *Egils saga Skalla-Grimssonar,* his significance for the development of the sagas of native heroes is even more striking. Paradoxically enough, the development of saga style to full perfection during the thirteenth century was of such a nature as to lend the works a more spoken or oral tone. It is obviously this disciplined and refined naturalness of language which has deceived modern readers and caused them to see nothing but oral tradition and oral narrative art in the sagas.

With such a concept of the sagas, Nordal naturally enough is no longer inclined to place so much weight on the historical and cultural traditions in this literature. In the program for future saga research which he sketches at the conclusion of his treatise on *Hrafnkatla,* he demands that one distinguish clearly between "the sagas' antiquarian ballast, the dead scholarship, and their eternally living soul: their excellence of style and narrative art, their character portrayal, their knowledge of human nature, and their views on life."[10]

CHAPTER 6

Style and Character Delineation

THE LITERARY PROSE of the Icelandic sagas is the oldest narrative prose known in any Scandinavian language. This prose is not absolutely uniform, even if one limits his criticism to the sagas of native heroes. A detailed investigation would doubtless reveal a considerable number of individual traits in style and diction. But in general this body of literature, viewed stylistically, has an unusually homogeneous character. It can, therefore, scarcely be regarded as an impermissible simplification if the Sagas of Icelanders are treated from this point of view as a uniform group.

What probably strikes the modern reader first of all in the language of the sagas is their simple, lucid sentence structure, which contrasts sharply with the artistic periods, strongly influenced by Latin, found in some of the translated works. Typical saga style avoids poetic embellishment. Andreas Heusler states that it would grate on one if he read in a saga: "He drew his *sharp* sword." The saga would have to express it thus: "He drew his sword; it was a sharp weapon."[1] The phraseology of the first sentence would be more suitable in the style of the ballad, with its more decorative manner of expression and its predilection for conventional epithets. The formulation of the second sentence is strictly objective, without poetic or emotional stress. Nor does the style of the sagas show any striving for variation in choice of words.[2] In several respects it is thus diametrically opposed to the diction of older and contemporary skalds. These poets were consistent in their endeavor to avoid conventional designations for things, and their sentence structure and word order were not infrequently of such a nature as to make the skaldic stanza into a sort of labyrinth. This may well be the fundamental reason why still today in Iceland a uniquely sharp distinction is made between poets and prose writers; even in works on modern Icelandic literature prose and poetry are preferably treated in separate chapters.[3]

Nature description for the purpose of creating a mood is almost completely lacking in the Sagas of Icelanders. Natural phenomena are usually mentioned only to the extent that they have significance for the action: the state of the weather or of the paths or roads, the moonlight which lights up the darkness of the night, and things of that sort.[4] As an extremely rare example of a more esthetic feeling for landscape, one may cite the famous words of Gunnarr of Hlíðarendi when, doomed to banishment from the country, he turned back when he had almost reached the ship which was to take him abroad: "Fair is the hillside. It has never seemed so fair to me before, with its fallow fields and mown hayfield. I will ride back home and never leave again."[5]

The saga writer shuns all effusive expression; indeed, he favors various striking forms of litotes, or understatement.[6] *Fóstbrœðra saga,* for example, relates that Þorgeirr, then fifteen years of age, late at night comes home to his mother after just having avenged the slaying of his father. His mother asks him if anything new had happened. The son answers: "A man was injured in Seljabrekka this evening." What has actually happened is that Þorgeirr thrust his spear right through the farmer on his own farm. In *Gísla saga Súrssonar* the outlawed hero slew one of the two men who were pursuing him in the forest. The other pursuer turned back to his comrades and greeted them with the comment that the going in the forest was rather difficult.

As a whole, the style of the sagas creates an impression of coolness and reserve. The narrator conceals his own presence, and this can create the impression that the story is relating itself. Epic objectivity is scrupulously observed. A typical case may be cited from *Droplaugarsona saga.* The widow Droplaug has married the widower Hallsteinn. It is expressly stated that her oldest son Helgi was opposed to the marriage. One autumn he comes to visit his mother on his stepfather's farm, Viðivellir. Droplaug asks Hallsteinn to invite Helgi to stay with them for the winter. Although reluctant to do so, the husband accedes to her wishes and Helgi accepts the invitation. The saga continues:

> Hallsteinn had a thrall named Þorgils. Two weeks after this, Helgi, Droplaug, and Þorgils had a long talk together; but no one else heard their conversation. During the winter Þorgils had the job of looking after the sheep in an enclosure south of the home-field, and he was a competent worker. He transported a great deal of hay to the enclosure.
>
> One day Þorgils came to Hallsteinn and asked him to come and take a look at the hay and the sheep. Hallsteinn went with him and entered the shed. When he was about to leave by way of a window, Þorgils struck him with an axe that belonged to Helgi Droplaugarson, and that blow was enough to kill him.
>
> Helgi was coming up the slope from his horses and arrived on the spot to see that Hallsteinn was dead. Helgi slew the thrall immediately. He went home and told his mother the news as she sat by the fire with the other women.
>
> Shortly afterward, people heard from members of the household at Viðivellir that Helgi, Droplaug, and Þorgils had talked for a long time together on the day before Hallsteinn was killed. And this slaying was ill spoken of. (Chap. 7.)

In such a passage one can speak of objectivity in a double sense. Everything indicates that mother and son agreed to have Hallsteinn slain and to use the thrall as an instrument in carrying this out; in turn the thrall was also killed, obviously to prevent him from revealing the truth of the matter. But this is not directly stated. The narrator leaves it to the hearer or reader to draw his own conclusions from the facts as stated. This very manner of presentation in the form of a neutral report naturally strengthens to a high degree the impression that one here has to do with an authentic series of events. But the narrator is also objective in a second sense: he does not permit himself to make a moral value judgment of the deed; he neither approves nor condemns it. On the other hand, there is nothing to prevent the characters of the saga themselves from giving expression to such an appraisement: "this slaying was ill spoken of." Naturally, this gives the author the possibility of masking his own judgment in the form of public opinion.

The characteristic traits of saga style probably best come into their own in the delineation of character. Character portrayal is, after all, the alpha and omega of this literary genre, which so often takes on the form of charged dialogues. Terse utterances and rejoinders can fall with fateful weight and sharpness, as in the famous conversation between Gunnarr of Hlíðarendi and his wife Hallgerðr, just before he is overcome by an overwhelmingly large band of men who are attacking him on his farm. One of his enemies has succeeded in surprising Gunnarr and cutting off the string to his bow. Without that weapon his chances of holding off the attackers and saving his life are greatly diminished:

"Take two strands of your hair," he said to Hallgerðr, "and you and mother twist it into a bowstring for me."

"Does it mean much to you?" asked Hallgerðr.

"It means my life," he replied. "For as long as I can use my bow, they won't be able to overpower me."

"In that case," she said, "I just now remember the slap in the face you gave me, and I don't care whether you defend yourself long or not."

"Everyone has his own way of gaining fame," said Gunnarr. "I won't ask this of you again."

73

"You are acting shamefully," said Rannveig, "and your disgrace will long be remembered." (Chap. 77.)

In this brief exchange of words, one of the high points of *Njála*, is concentrated much of the essence of the Icelandic saga. Here is easily injured pride, which finds uncanny expression in Hallgerðr's overwrought desire for revenge. Here is the typical self-control of the hero in the hour of his fate, preferably accentuated by an ironic or sarcastic catchword or rejoinder. Gunnarr's reply to his wife regarding the various ways of attaining fame reveals the saga characters' keen appreciation of posthumous renown and honor, of the good repute of dead men which, according to Hávamál, never dies.[7] This same attitude is expressed more straightforwardly by Rannveig's prophecy of her daughter-in-law's shame.

The author's direct presentation of a character when introduced into the story usually consists of quite stereotyped formulations. Of a woman it may be stated summarily that she was of pleasing appearance; possibly her blond hair is mentioned as an example of her beauty. It may further be said regarding her that she is an efficient housekeeper, that she is a woman of temperament, that she is versed in magic lore, and the like. (The fact that Kormákr in the saga which bears his name should especially praise the feet of his adored Steingerðr may perhaps be attributed to his special sensitivity or originality as a poet!) On the other hand, the appearance and qualities of a man are not infrequently described in a more diversified manner, with details about his hair, nose, mouth, stature. In certain cases such a description is reserved with artistic calculation for a crucial moment in the story, when it casts an especially strong light on the figure in question. An example of this is the description of Egill Skalla-Grímsson in the hall of King Ethelstan following the battle in which his older brother Þórólfr was killed. In the hall there is boisterous merriment and high glee. Egill takes the place assigned him on the seat of honor directly opposite the king. He sits down and casts his shield in front of his feet:

> He had his helmet on his head and laid his sword across his knees. He kept drawing the sword halfway out of the sheath and thrusting it back in again. He sat upright, but his head was bowed. Egill had coarse features: a broad forehead, bushy eyebrows, and a short and extremely thick nose. His long beard covered much of his face, and his chin and jawbone were terribly broad. His neck was so thick and his shoulders so broad that he stood out from all other men. His expression was harsh and grim when he was angry. He was of great stature, being taller than anyone else. His hair was gray and thick, but he became bald quite young. But as he sat there, as here described, he alternately pulled one of his eyebrows down to his cheek and the other one up to his hairline. Egill had black eyes and eyebrows. He would not drink, even though he had been served, but continued to raise and lower his eyebrows. (Chap. 55.)

Thereupon it is described how the king, with the help of rich gifts of gold and silver, is able to get Egill back into a good mood again.[8]

This plastic portrait occurs at a decisive point in the story. Actually it is only now, approximately at mid-point in the saga, that Egill in every respect really emerges as the chief character; previously he was somewhat put into the background by the resplendent figure of his admired older brother. Thus Egill is presented in a full-length portrait just at the time when he is on the point of assuming his role as the completely dominating person in the story.[9]

Such a direct description in connection with a definite occasion is, of course, not the only or even the most important method of characterization in the sagas. Generally the character of the individual is slowly revealed through a long series of situations and conversations in the interplay among people of diverse personalities. In comparison with the psychological fiction of a later period, the portrayal of the characters' deeper motives, thoughts, and feelings in the sagas may impress one as meager. On the whole, the saga people are depicted from without, in their demeanor, actions, and words, or in the judgment of others. This artistic economy of means is so great that the modern reader may easily miss certain psychological connections. An example can be cited from the above-quoted *Droplaugarsona saga*.

Helgi Droplaugarson has been killed in a fight. About his younger brother, who was seriously wounded on the same occasion but escaped death, the saga relates: "Grímr remained for several years in Krossavík and was depressed; he never laughed after Helgi had been killed." Finally, Grímr is able on an expedition with a few trusted friends to get at his chief adversary and slay him in his bed. He and his companions escape their pursuers in the darkness and are soon back at Krossavík again. People ask them the news, but they say that they have nothing to report. On the following day Grímr is playing chess with a Norwegian who happens to be there on a visit. A boy, the son of the farmer Þorkell and his wife Jórunn, bumps into the table and upsets the pieces. "The Norwegian took a kick at the boy, and the startled lad broke wind. Grímr roared with laughter. Then Jórunn went over to him and said: 'What actually did happen on your trip last night, and what report have you brought back?' " In reply Grímr quotes several verses which clear up the matter for her.

When the modern reader comes to the place where Grímr bursts out laughing, it is not at all certain that he will associate this with the statement made five pages earlier that Grímr had not laughed since the slaying of his brother. Perhaps one might even consider the episode bizarre and puzzling, a peculiarly unfitting addition to the story. But the housewife of Krossavík immediately draws the right conclusion from the laughter of Grímr. Obviously the author of the saga mentioned the boy's little mishap just for the purpose of giving Grímr some reason for laughing. From the very beginning he intended that this scene should relate to the previous statement about Grímr's gloominess.

Such an extreme economy in psychological motivation requires alertness and close attention on the part of the reader for a clear understanding of the context of the story. But it would be a mistake to interpret this as a primitive narrative technique or as a lack of sensitivity on the part of the author. On the contrary, the artistic effects are often very finely calculated. And the variety and individuality of the persons portrayed can be quite amazing.

In *Njála*, for instance, men and women from all classes of society are depicted. A whole line of chieftains march by, each with his own individual stamp; some of them are portrayed with biting sarcasm by Skarpheðinn during the "supplication journey" of Njáll's sons at the General Assembly. In this saga there are also, to be sure, many ordinary farmers, servants, herdsmen, freedmen, and thralls. Wandering old beggarwomen contribute to the progress of the narrative by carrying gossip and tales from farm to farm. Among the members of the household at Bergþórshváll we meet the old woman Sæunn, who, although in her second childhood, is prescient and conscious of the fact that Njáll and her foster daughter Bergþóra will be burned to death in their house. A touching contrast to this old woman is provided by little Þórðr, who wants to share the fate of his grandmother Bergþóra and of Njáll: " 'But you promised me, Grandmother, that we two would never be parted, and that's the way it shall be,' said the boy. 'I would much rather die with the both of you than to live after you.' Thereupon she carried the boy to their bed." Then there is the somber, sarcastic, and somewhat frightening figure of the warrior Skarpheðinn. Beside him stand heroes of a lighter disposition: around Gunnarr and Kári there is an aura of the ideal of chivalry. In his impetuous and sometimes impulsive actions Skarpheðinn is also a contrast to his father, the wise and peaceable Njáll. The saga has room for both good and evil characters. Through the manner of his death Höskuldr Hvítanesgoði acquires something of the faint, tremulous light of a martyr. He falls as an innocent victim of fateful slander, cunningly spread about by Mörðr, the real villain of the drama. There is also a more obvious scoundrel named Hrappr, as he himself quite objectively admits. In Kári and his weapon-bearer Björn from Mörk the author of this saga has described with subtle humor the contrasting interplay between a matter-of-fact courageous warrior and a chicken-hearted braggart. It is clear, too, that the characters of Hallgerðr and Bergþóra have been drawn with artistic design as contrasts. During the attack on Hlíðarendi, Hallgerðr with cold-blooded, malignant vengefulness leaves her fighting mate in the lurch, whereas Bergþóra at the burning of Bergþórshváll without hesitation chooses to share the fate of her husband.

The sharp contours and the plasticity of saga style clearly make it a very effective instrument in the hands of a skillful narrator. Scandinavian writers of later times—not infrequently the greatest of them—have time and again turned back to the Icelandic sagas in an effort to temper their own styles.

From time to time people have noticed the similarity between saga style and the so-called hard-boiled narrative technique of our own day as represented, for example, by Ernest Hemingway.[10] And the points of agreement are striking. On both sides the chief emphasis is on the depiction of tangible external facts. One records observable reactions instead of making psychological analysis. Dialogue, preferably carried out in short utterances and cutting repartee, plays an important role. The objective attitude can create the impression of indifference or cynicism.

As far as is known, there is no direct connection between the Sagas of Icelanders and the modern hard-boiled genre. But people have sought to derive the similarities from certain common features in the physiognomy of the times, then and now. The Age of the Sturlungs in Iceland, during which the sagas were written, has already been characterized. Christianity had long since been introduced officially, but its spirit had not yet been able to permeate the Icelanders' view of life. Moral values wavered uncertainly in the gap between two systems of norms. The political situation acquired its impress from the ruthless feuds between powerful chieftains. No one could be sure of life and limb; peril lurked in all quarters, even from one's own kinsmen. In such an age it was dangerous to cling to illusions. Men's attitudes became sober and skeptical. It is this mode of thought and conduct to which saga style has given ultimate expression.

On the other hand, attempts have been made to relate the hard-boiled narrative style to the First World War. All earlier life ideals were shattered, without being replaced by new ones. People remained skeptical and could no longer view life from a definite moral point of view. One had to accept brutal reality as it was. That there actually is a connection between the world war and Hemingway's style could perhaps be illustrated by a commentary from his novel *A Farewell to Arms* (1929). The narrator states that he always becomes embarrassed when he hears words such as "sacred" or "sacrifice." In the war nothing was sacred, and its sacrifices made one think of the slaughter houses in Chicago. Talk about honor, courage, and similar things finally appeared obscene in comparison with the names of towns and rivers and the numbers of roads and army divisions. This disgust at anything except the tangible is clearly a presupposition of the hard-boiled style with its connection with quipping journalistic prose or the language of objective communication.

In spite of all this, of course, the difference between Iceland during the Sturlung Age and Europe or America during the First World War is enormous. The similarity between saga style and its modern counterpart is perhaps also not quite so profound as it may appear at first glance. Whereas the coldly objective attitude of the sagas produces the effect of naturalness, it seems in the prose of our day to be more like the manifestation of a violent reaction against sentimentality and ineffective, impotent idealism. For this reason the hard-boiled narrative style not infrequently has a trace of hysteria which is foreign to saga style, with its calmly matter-of-course, epic authority. Nor does one find in more recent literature the soberly objective manner of presentation carried out with a consistency which even approaches the Icelandic sagas, except possibly in rare exceptional cases.

The style of the Sagas of Icelanders appears to be a unique phenomenon, and later attempts to revive its artistic effectiveness have seldom turned out well. This style was and will always remain an expression of a particular nation during a particular time in its history, an expression of its ideals, its view of man, and its artistic aspirations.

CHAPTER 7

Dreams and Destiny

No READER OF THE Icelandic sagas can fail to notice the great significance of the dreams which occur in them; it has been estimated that there are on the average three or four dreams per saga. This is due in large measure to the fact that dreams often become bearers of the belief in fate which marks the saga people's view of life. Not infrequently a person's fate is revealed in his own dreams or in those of others.

The dream as a literary motif is known from all ages and among all peoples. This is not difficult to understand when one considers the similarity of dreams to the capricious visions of fantasy or the fabrications of fairy tales. These constitute a world which is completely independent of the usual laws of logic and causality. Dreams captivate one because they are full of mysteries and enigmas. There is more meaning to them than meets the eye.

In ancient times—in the Semitic and Graeco-Roman cultures as well as among the early Germanic peoples—there existed a belief in dreams supported by the people's religion and their general view of the world. The singular significance of dreams was based on the belief that they were infused into the minds of men by supernatural powers. Such dreams had to be accorded special weight. Properly interpreted, they could foretell the future, reveal one's destiny. In the literatures of ancient times the dream was usually in the form of a prophecy, and this prophetic character was long retained in literary dream depictions. This attitude toward dreams has persisted in popular belief to this very day. On the other hand, dreams, as is well known, have assumed quite a different import according to modern interpretation. Under the influence primarily of psychoanalysis one no longer regards the dream as a revelation of impending fate, but as an emanation or projection of the dreamer's own psyche. The dark forces of the subconscious are given free play when the controls and inhibitions of the conscious are relaxed. Wishes and complexes which the individual is unwilling to acknowledge when awake are revealed in artful disguises in dreams.

Obviously one cannot regard the dreams of the Icelandic sagas in the light of psychoanalytic dream interpretation. In this body of literature dreams are artistically exploited precisely as they were in ancient times for the purpose of indicating coming events. As a rule, the dreams in the sagas are of the kind that forbode misfortune; they usually predict strife and death. Often they are quite stereotyped in content and construction. A common example is that of an enemy who appears in the form of a dangerous animal. At least in several cases it is clear that animal figures were regarded as attendant or protective spirits (*fylgjur*) of the persons referred to.

In *Droplaugarsona saga* one of the chief characters has an unpleasant dream which he relates rather late the following day to one of his companions:

> "It seemed to me," said Helgi, "as though we were riding along the same path we are traveling now, and were going down along Eyvindardalr to Kálfshváll. Suddenly eighteen or twenty wolves came rushing toward us, and one of them was much larger than the rest. We tried to get to the hill but couldn't. They attacked us at once, and one of them tore my chin and teeth, and then I woke up." (Chap. 10.)

Helgi's companion is ready at once to interpret the dream. Somewhere along the way men are lying in ambush for Helgi; their leader is the chieftain Helgi Ásbjarnarson. In spite of this warning Helgi refuses to change his course, and the dream comes true in every respect. Helgi and his followers are attacked from ambush by a band of eighteen men led by Helgi Ásbjarnarson. Even the detail of the dream about the wolf's ripping open Helgi's jaw and the front of his mouth has its counterpart in reality. Before Helgi finally goes down, he parries a blow with his shield. His opponent's sword glances off into Helgi's face, strikes the front teeth, and shears off the lower lip.

Many more examples could be cited of dreams which relate to definite events or episodes, to conflicts, slayings, etc. Less frequently, a dream or a series of dreams is used to foreshadow a longer course of action. An example of this is found in *Gunnlaugs saga ormstungu,* in which Þorsteinn's dream at the very beginning indicates the way in which future events will develop. In this dream the vision of the bloody battle of the two eagles for the female swan symbolizes the conflict between Gunnlaugr and Hrafn for Helga in fagra. The arrival of the falcon after the death of the eagles and his departure with the swan signifies the marriage of Helga to another man.

During the winter before her first wedding Guðrún Ósvífrsdóttir in *Laxdæla saga* has four different dreams which predict the outcome of her four marriages. She cannot interpret the dreams herself and has no idea what they refer to. In order to get help in explaining them, she turns to the chieftain Gestr, "a wise man who could often see into the future." Every one of the dreams deals with a certain object, a concrete thing.

In her third dream Guðrún had put a golden band on her arm. This seemed to her to be a replacement for a lost silver band—a dream symbol for her second husband, still alive, who was to drown. But she did not feel that it adorned her better to the extent that gold is more precious than silver. She dreamed further that she fell down and thrust forth her hand. The golden armband struck against a stone and broke in two, and blood ran from both pieces. She recalled that there had been a flaw in the band before. And now when she examined the pieces, she thought she saw more cracks. She had a feeling that the ornament might still be unbroken if she had taken better care of it. According to Gestr, this band signified that Guðrún would marry a third time, but her third husband would not surpass her second one in proportion to the extent that gold is more precious than silver. Gestr has a premonition that in time a new religious faith will come to Iceland and that Guðrún's future husband will embrace this faith, which will be regarded as higher and better than the old one. The fact that the armband was broken, partly because of Guðrún's own lack of care, and that blood flowed from the pieces means that this husband will be slain. In the course of the story Guðrún marries Bolli, who, with his kinsman and foster brother Kjartan, has been baptized in Norway. But it is really Kjartan whom Guðrún loves, and Bolli won her with somewhat misleading reports about his foster brother while he was abroad. This situation develops into a triangle drama which is strongly reminiscent of that between Helga and Gunnlaugr and Hrafn in *Gunnlaugs saga ormstungu*. An exact interpretation of the meaning of the cracks in the armband in Guðrún's dream is difficult. It is conceivable that they are intended as allusions to certain flaws in Bolli's character, to his lack of sincerity which was to have dire consequences. More probably they refer to the unstable relationship between Bolli and Kjartan and their kinsmen which resulted from Bolli's marriage with Guðrún. Bolli is relentlessly incited by his wife to kill Kjartan. When finally he reluctantly commits this heinous crime against his foster brother, he himself is slain in vengeance and falls before Kjartan's brothers. Thus Guðrún must be said to have had a part in Bolli's death just as Gestr interpreted her dream about the broken and bleeding armband.

It is not necessary to discuss Guðrún's fourth dream and its interpretation, except to mention that it, too, ended in a death by drowning, just like the second one. Characteristically enough, still another, lesser dream figures in the description of how Guðrún's fourth dream was fulfilled. She was married for a number of years to the powerful chieftain Þorkell Eyjólfsson. He once dreams that his beard grew so long that it extended over the Breiðafjörður. He asks Guðrún to interpret the dream. Guðrún asks him what he thinks it means. Þorkell interprets the dream as signifying that his power will one day encompass the entire Breiða-fjörður District.[1] "That is possible," replies Guðrún, "but I rather believe it means that you will dip your beard in the fjord." Through her own dream and Gestr's interpretation of it Guðrún already was prescient of Þorkell's end. She and the saga reader share this insight. When Þorkell, who is without this foreknowledge, now attributes an optimistic and somewhat presumptuous significance to his dream, the resulting effect is one of tragic irony.

In *Laxdæla* and *Gunnlaugs saga ormstungu* the dreams not only have a key position as a sort of symbolic summary of the entire central course of events; they also comprise a more complicated pattern than the simple dreams of attacking wolves and other savage beasts. Both of these sagas also reflect in dream descriptions the influence of a more romantic ideal of style than that which prevails in most of the sagas of native heroes. Þorsteinn's dream in *Gunnlaugs saga ormstungu* is probably modeled on that of Kriemhild in the *Nibelungenlied*. Both of them involve two eagles and a falcon, and in both works the falcon stands for the man to whom the woman is married. In *Laxdæla saga* one observes that the symbolic objects Guðrún dreams about in two instances are armbands of silver and gold and in the fourth case a golden helmet set with precious stones. That is quite characteristic of this saga, which also in other ways reveals a special fondness for chivalric splendor.

In *Gísla saga Súrssonar* dreams play an uncommonly dominant and quite unique role. It is said of the chief character, among other things, that he was "a wise man, and one who had many prophetic dreams." A subtle touch in this saga—which, incidentally, is remarkable in several respects—is that it does not make the dreams a real force in Gísli's existence until he has been outlawed for manslaughter. In this situation his brooding about his own future cannot but be intensified with manifold force. The enforced loneliness increases his receptivity to the suggestions of the dreams. One autumn, when Gísli was staying secretly on his farm with his wife Auðr, who had faithfully aided him during his outlawry, he slept fitfully. When he awoke, Auðr asked him what he had dreamed:

"There are two women in my dreams," he said. "One of them is kind to me, but the other one always tells me things that seem worse than before, and she prophesies nothing but misfortune for me. Just now I dreamed that I was going up to a house or to a hall, and I thought I went into the house, and there I recognized many people, kinsmen and friends of mine. They were sitting by the fires drinking, and there were seven fires. Some of them were almost burned down, but the others were burning very brightly. Then my good dream woman came in and told me they signified the time I still had left to live. And she advised me, while I was alive, to renounce the old faith and never to learn sorcery and pagan lore, but always to be kind to the deaf and the lame, and to the poor and helpless. That is all the longer the dream was." (Chap. 22.)

This experience of an evil and a good dream woman recurs regularly from now on in Gísli's dreams. Sometimes it is the evil one and sometimes it is the good one which has the most to say to him. It is especially during autumn, when the nights begin to grow longer, that the dream visions beset Gísli. One autumn, for instance, he dreams frequently that the evil woman comes to him and wants to wash him in blood. Finally, when the seven years are past which were allotted him in the dream about the seven fires, and he is approaching his impending death, Gísli's horrible dreams reach their culmination. As soon as he closes his eyes, he is harassed by blood-dripping visions, the work of the evil dream woman. He becomes fearful of the dark and does not dare remain alone anywhere. Yet, he rises to the occasion and acquits himself heroically in his final battle against an overwhelming number of enemies.

As has been stated, the dreams in the Icelandic sagas must not be conceived of primarily as psychological, as the expression of the dreamer's emotional state, but rather as something implanted in a man's mind from without, by some mysterious force outside of himself. On the other hand, dreams occur above all among such persons who have a special occasion for concern about their fate. The foremost example of this is Gísli Súrsson. The modern reader has a strong impression that the dualism in Gísli's dreams directly reflects the struggle within his soul between hope and fear—even though the author of the saga may not consciously have conceived of the matter in this way.[2]

As already indicated, there is a close connection between dreams and destiny in the Sagas of Icelanders. *Laxdæla* and *Gísla saga Súrssonar* do not merely yield some of the best examples of dreams; they are also based on a pronounced fatalism. The dream serves as a means of giving artistic form to this belief in fate. But this is also expressed in many other ways. Indeed, fatalism is one of the essential elements in the world of the Icelandic saga. In many cases it supplies the key to an understanding of people's words and deeds, and of their image of themselves and of each other. As A. U. Bååth has stated, the belief in fate runs through the sagas like a red string and a principle of composition, and not least of all through the most artistic and best constructed ones.[3]

It may not be immediately clear what the terms destiny and fatalism actually mean. To begin with, one must draw a clear line of demarcation between fatalism and religion. One may speak of religion when people trust in the ability of divine power to fulfill their desires and in the efficacy of their own prayers and sacrifices to influence the course of future events. If, however, they are dominated by fatalism, they conceive of their existence as ruled by inescapable and immutable necessity. If one were to try by some sort of magic performance or incantation to exert an influence on his destiny, that would in fact mean that one did not really regard that destiny as destiny in the strict meaning of the word. Under the guise of the powers of fate one would then be worshiping spirits or gods which would be regarded as accessible to human desires. True fate or destiny must be accepted absolutely without reservation.

It is obvious that a consistent fatalism must have important consequences for the moral judgment of human beings. The coldly objective portrayal of people in the Sagas of Icelanders, which as a rule refrains from all ethical evaluations in our sense of the word, appears to be closely connected with this fatalism. That does not mean, however, that the saga characters and the saga writers were without a moral standard. It is by his attitude toward his fate more than in any other way that a saga character can prove his mettle. He can succumb to his fate, broken and resigned, or he can meet it unbroken and with heroic affirmation. Here is where he reveals his worth as a man and establishes his own renown: the judgment by posterity of a dead man.

The best way to obtain a good concept of how fatalism manifests itself in the world of the Icelandic sagas is to examine several sagas individually.

When Þorsteinn Egilsson in *Gunnlaugs saga ormstungu* is frightened by his dream about the swan, the eagles, and the falcon, he orders that a still unborn child is to be exposed to die in case it is a girl. By this command he believes that he has brought to nought the prophecy of the dream. But his wife gives birth to the child during his absence and provides for its safety. And when Þorsteinn six years later learns the truth, he is reconciled with what has happened and in commenting on it says: "In most cases, things turn out as they must" (literally, "they roll where they want to"). When the first duel between the rivals Gunnlaugr and Hrafn ends indecisively, the relatives of the two realize that they will not be able to prevent them from resuming the combat in Norway. (After the holmgang between Gunnlaugr and Hrafn this sort of contest, according to the saga, was forbidden by law in Iceland.) The intention of the two men to meet again abroad is accompanied by the words: "Their kinsmen on both sides were greatly disturbed at this, but they could do nothing about it because the two were so vehement and, after all, what was decreed has to come to pass" (literally, "that had to be forthcoming which was drawing near"). This implies, therefore, that both Gunnlaugr and Hrafn had to fall in combat. Events "roll" or "draw onward" toward their completion—without any interference from supernatural, mysterious powers. Destiny, the inexorable course of human events, seems to rest partly in the character of the individual concerned and partly in external circumstances. The saga's concept of human nature is decidedly deterministic.

The main action in *Laxdæla saga*, as already mentioned, centers upon Guðrún Ósvífrsdóttir and the two kinsmen and foster brothers, Kjartan and Bolli. Kjartan comes from an aristocratic family which is said to be endowed with *gipta* or *hamingja*, two Icelandic words for the "good fortune" or "success" which is given to a family or to an individual. (The word *gipta* is etymologically related to the verb *to give* and therefore refers to something which has been given or allotted to one.) But this good fortune is never constant. Wise and prescient Gestr foresees that Kjartan will be slain by his foster brother Bolli and that Bolli, in turn, will be killed for this deed. "It is uncanny," Gestr admits to his son, "to know this in advance of two such remarkable men."

After Guðrún's first two marriages she and Kjartan grow fond of each other. Furthermore their fathers, Ósvífr and Óláfr, have long been united in close friendship. But Kjartan's father has dark premonitions, which he reveals to his son:

"I do not know," he said, "why I always become depressed when you go to Laugar to visit Guðrún. It is not because I do not regard Guðrún above all other women. . . . But I have a foreboding (*hugboð*), although I do not want to prophesy, that our kinsmen and the people at Laugar will not have any good fortune (*gæfa*) from our dealings with each other." (Chap. 39.)

Bolli and Kjartan both sail to Norway, where King Óláfr Tryggvason, after considerable persuasion, succeeds in getting them to accept baptism. Kjartan is among the Icelanders whom the king selects to remain in Norway as hostages until Christianity is accepted in Iceland. Bolli, on the other hand, is permitted to go back. He now succeeds in winning Guðrún for himself. She is very unyielding, however, and complies only after he has convinced her that there is slight prospect of Kjartan's return.

But when Christianity is finally accepted in Iceland, Kjartan receives permission to leave the Norwegian court—where he has enjoyed great honor and popularity—and to go aboard his ship. King Óláfr gazed after him and said: "Hard things are destined for Kjartan and his kinsmen, and it will not be easy for them to avert their fate (*forlög*)."

After Kjartan's return home he tries to establish a friendly relationship with Guðrún and Bolli. He also gets married. In this situation, however, Guðrún's former love for Kjartan turns to hate—or in any case is manifested as such—and she incites her brothers to kill him. The tragedy is greatly intensified because on top of everything she eggs on her husband Bolli, Kjartan's foster brother, to take part in the deed. In reply to his objections she says cynically: "What you say is true, but it was not granted you (*eigi*

muntu bera giptu) to act in such a way as to please every-
body. And if you hold back now, our life together is over."
Near the place where Kjartan and his opponents meet,
there are a shepherd boy and the farmer for whom he works.
The boy catches sight of both parties, the men from Laugar
in their place of ambush, and Kjartan, who is riding along
with only two companions. He wants to run and warn
Kjartan, but the farmer stops him. "Hold your tongue! Do
you think, you simpleton, that you can lengthen a man's
life if he is fated to die!" (Icelandic *ef bana verðr auðit*,
"if death is destined"; this word *auðit*, which is the perfect
participle of an otherwise obsolete verb, is the source of the
Swedish word *öde*, "fate.")

When the opponents come to blows, Bolli keeps out of
the conflict as long as possible. But he is urged to fight by
his comrades, who are unable to defeat Kjartan without
him; and he finally draws his sword and deals the death
blow to his exhausted and resigned foster brother. This deed
of Bolli, carried out reluctantly and immediately regretted,
is the great misfortune of his life, his *óhapp*, to use the
word of the saga. And it also leads to his own death at the
hands of Kjartan's brothers.

The events which revolve around Guðrún have been
shaped into the form of a gradual waning of people's good
fortune, which was foreseen and predicted by certain persons. Fate does not appear as a kind of *deus ex machina*
which suddenly reveals itself and turns the course of events
into a certain direction. On the contrary, the development
of the action, at least from a modern point of view, is quite
adequately motivated in the characters of the persons themselves, especially in that of Guðrún. At the same time, one
must grant that the many premonitions and dreams definitely point to the existence of some impersonal power which
exists outside of the people but steers the course of events
through them. But in such a case this force is not providence but cold, inexorable necessity.

91

Clearly and deliberately *Gísla saga Súrssonar* was designed by its author to make the reader perceive that the course of events is determined by fate. This immediately becomes evident upon the examination of several key episodes.

During a spring assembly the so-called Haukdælir (the people of the Haukadalur in the region of the Dýrafjörður) were sitting together in complete amity at a drinking bout. But wise Gestr—the same prescient man who appears in *Laxdæla saga*—predicted that three years hence not everyone in this group would be as completely in accord with the rest as they were then. It was also known that there was a certain amount of discord among the Haukdælir, even if it had not yet become critical. Gísli, who of all the people of Haukadalur was most keenly aware of what appeared to be in store for them, wanted to do everything possible to prevent Gestr's prediction from becoming true. To this end, he proposed that the kinsmen enter a pact of sworn brotherhood for the purpose of strengthening the solidarity among them. This was to include four men: the brothers Gísli and Þorkell and their brothers-in-law Þorgrímr and Vésteinn. Þorgrímr was married to Þórdís, the sister of Gísli and Þorkell, and Gísli was married to Auðr, the sister of Vésteinn. At this ceremony they were to swear an oath that each of them would avenge any of the others as his brother, and they were to name all of the gods as witnesses to this oath. But when they joined hands, Þorgrímr declared that he had assumed sufficient responsibility by entering into this pact with his brothers-in-law, Þorkell and Gísli. He did not regard himself as obligated to Vésteinn in any way—and with that he drew back his hand from him. Then Gísli behaved in the same way toward Þorgrímr: he was unwilling to undertake any responsibilities in regard to one who refused to stand firmly behind his brother-in-law Vésteinn. And thus, contrary to Gísli's intent, the result of his proposal was that the weak spots in the relationship of the four men to each other were immediately clearly revealed. Afterward he also said to his brother: "Now things have turned out as I suspected; and what has just been done will be of no avail. And I believe that now fate will decide this matter."

For Gísli it is now of the greatest urgency to protect his beloved brother-in-law and sworn-brother Vésteinn from lurking dangers. Once, when they are to be separated during a voyage abroad, Gísli makes a metal disc in two halves which fit together perfectly. He keeps one piece and gives the other one to Vésteinn. These are to be sent as a message between the two brothers-in-law if the life of either of them should be threatened. Gísli's *hugr* tells him that they will some day be in such a position.

Fate is not long in making itself felt. Gísli and his brother Þorkell own a farm in common. One day Þorkell happens to overhear a conversation between his wife Ásgerðr and his brother's wife Auðr. Auðr reproaches her sister-in-law for having an affair with Vésteinn, and Ásgerðr does not deny that she is more fond of Vésteinn than of her own husband. Auðr is frightened when it is discovered that Þorkell has heard what she said. She goes to Gísli and asks him not to be angry with her and to try to devise some plan:

> "I cannot think of a plan that would be of any use," said Gísli, "and yet I cannot blame you for what happened; for someone had to speak the words of fate (*sköp*), and what is destined will come to pass." (Chap. 9.)

Þorkell, who up to that time has been living like a parasite from his brother's work on the farm without himself lifting a hand to help, now wishes to divide up the estate. In spite of the fact that Gísli personally would stand to benefit by such an arrangement, he opposes it. His feeling of family integrity is very strong, and he knows that putting an end to their common ownership of this property can weaken this solidarity within the family. But Þorkell succeeds in having his way and moves to the farm of his brother-in-law Þorgrímr, which is just a short distance away. With this the crack in the originally intended state of sworn brotherhood has further widened. The outlines of a threat against Vésteinn now clearly emerge. To be sure, the injured husband Þorkell himself is still bound by his oath; but Þorgrímr is free to seek vengeance on his behalf.

When Gísli learns that Vésteinn has returned to Iceland from his voyage abroad, he at once sends messengers to meet him with his half of the metal disc. But it so happens that Vésteinn is riding along another road from that on which the messengers expected to meet him; they do not overtake him until he has almost reached his destination, and then he can no longer be held back. If they had happened to meet him sooner, he would have turned back. "But from here all the rivers flow into the Dýrafjörður, and I, too, shall ride there." This picture of the streaming water courses is a magnificent symbol of the irrevocability of fate, perhaps the most splendid in the entire body of saga literature.

When the messengers return to Gísli with their report, he merely says: "That is the way it must be." He has done what he could to block the course of fate, but in the end he appears to be resigned to it. It now seems to him as if everything were "pointing in the same direction" (*einn veg á horfask*). Even when Vésteinn as a guest in Gísli's house is pierced through by a spear in bed at night, the host remains strangely passive, although he must have had a premonition of the deed just before it was committed. At first glance it might almost seem as though Gísli has now placed himself of his own free will in the service of the inevitable.

After Vésteinn's death it is Gísli's turn to strike. The murder was committed in secret, but the relationship between the men being what it was, one need have no doubts as to who the slayer is. Gísli carries out his vengeance against Þorgrímr cold-bloodedly and methodically and with a good conscience, since he is merely fulfilling the oath of sworn brotherhood. But with the same deed he also determines his own fate, for it leads to his outlawry and finally to his death.

It is impossible to apply an ethical standard of measurement to events of this kind. The outcome of it all can scarcely be said to bear witness to any kind of justice as a leading principle. Gísli is a right-minded and benevolent man, who from the very outset does more than anyone else to ward off the impending evil. One of the most disturbing experiences of the old saga writers appears to have been the recognition that worthy men, too, must endure suffering and defeat—merely because they lack a sufficient measure of "good fortune," of that life-furthering force for which the language has a number of designations: *gipta, gæfa, hamingja.* Such a man is the outlaw Gísli, against whom everything seems to have conspired. The only explanation given in the saga for his personal fate is that he is not a "man of good fortune" *(gæfumaðr).*

One might think that a fatalism such as that of the Icelandic sagas could lead to complete resignation and paralysis of action. But paradoxically enough this is not so at all. Gísli Súrsson ultimately knows quite well that he is a doomed man, and that his defense will not serve any practical purpose. In the summer night before his final battle he cuts runes into a stick as he walks along, and he lets the shavings fall on the ground, clearly for the purpose of showing his pursuers the way. His dreams have revealed to him that his end has come. But this certainly does not paralyze him; on the contrary, it seems to endow him with a kind of inner freedom and gladness. He defends himself with a magnificent will to fight, and is determined to inflict the greatest possible harm on his attackers. In a final stanza he pays tribute to his faithful wife and thanks his father for having given him as his heritage an uncompromising spirit. And a similar attitude is shown by a large number of heroic and ideal figures in the sagas. In the very last struggle, as it were, they affirm their own fate with the highest measure of clear-sightedness, vitality, and courage. This gives them in spite of everything a kind of proud independence; like the Greeks in Fröding's *Ur Anabasis* they refuse to be bowed "in fear and madness under their harsh fate." In this sense perhaps the saga authors have after all done full poetic justice to their heroes marked by misfortune. For it is primarily not fate, immutable and dark, which holds the attention of the reader, but rather the heroic attitude of the characters toward this fate—not defeat, but victory.

Actually no paradoxical contrast exists between the fatalism of the sagas and their heroic ideals. In the first place, it was not necessary to imagine that every single detail in a man's life is determined by fate. He could reckon with a range of freedom for the human will and human intervention within certain limits, which might be relatively wide or narrow. On the other hand, the people in the Icelandic sagas are not at all determined in their behavior by their relationship to metaphysical powers, but by their attitude toward other people and toward the existing code of honor. It is here that one must seek the basic motives of their conduct. And thus the question arises: What are the values in life which are esteemed most highly in the sagas?

CHAPTER 8

Life Values and Ideals

ONE OF THE CHIEF CHARACTERS in *Fóstbræðra saga,* Þormóðr, on a certain occasion has crawled down under a pile of seaweed on a little island in an attempt to escape his pursuers. However, a woman named Þórdís, who is leading the pursuit, suspects just this kind of trick. She orders her men servants to go up on the island and comb the seaweed by thrusting their spears into it, and to do this thoroughly and repeatedly. Þormóðr receives several wounds, but he does not betray his presence by a single sound or movement. The men servants return after their unsuccessful search. Then Þórdís says: "I believe that he is here on the island, even if you couldn't find him. Now, if Þormóðr can hear my words, let him answer me if he has the courage of a man and not that of a mare." When Þormóðr hears this, he wants to reply at once; faced with such an accusation of cowardice, he is ready to spoil his successful ruse and expose himself to certain death. But, according to the saga, he is unable to utter a sound: it is just as though someone were holding his hand over his mouth.

Another episode in the same saga related that the sworn-brothers Þormóðr and Þorgeirr together went to look for angelica on some cliffs by the sea. Suddenly the loose stones begin sliding under Þorgeirr's feet; just in the nick of time he manages to grasp a stalk of angelica with fairly strong roots. There he dangles now over the abyss, hundreds of feet above the rocky beach, with no possibility of pulling himself up and in danger of having the stalk he is clinging to give way at any moment. But it does not occur to him to call his sworn-brother, who is somewhat higher up on the slope. Rather, it is Þormóðr who, with no inkling of the situation, calls to his comrade and asks if he hasn't collected enough angelica. "Þorgeirr answered with a steady voice and a fearless heart: 'I think I shall have enough when the one I'm holding on to now pulls out.' " This sounds suspicious to Þormóðr. He discovers his sworn-brother's dangerous situation, climbs down, and succeeds in pulling him up just in time. No further words are wasted about the incident.

These are several examples of a pride which is intensified and vulnerable to such a degree that it sometimes strikes the modern reader as slightly comical. This heroic ideology stands out most sharply in especially dramatic situations, above all at the very moment of death. Then it is preferably crystallized out in the form of a grim laconic utterance. In the battle of Stiklastaðir, Þormóðr Kolbrúnar-skáld was struck right in the heart by an iron-tipped arrow. He has broken off the shaft of the arrow, and now a woman skilled in leechcraft is trying to pull out the iron arrowhead with a pair of tongs; she cannot dislodge it, however, because the wound has become so swollen that the arrowhead barely protrudes. Then Þormóðr asks the woman to cut away the flesh around the piece of iron, and he grasps the tongs himself. He wrenches out the arrowhead with its barb, to which adhere "shreds of the heart, some red, and others white, yellow, and green." When Þormóðr sees that, he remarks: "The king has fed us well; there is fat around the roots of my heart." He also recites an eight-line verse before he dies on his feet, leaning against a wall.

Grettir's brother Atli is scarcely inferior to Þormóðr in this respect. When he receives a spear thrust right through the middle of his body, he comments calmly: "The broad-bladed spear-points are in vogue now," and falls on his face over the doorsill. The record in heroic laconism is probably held by Vésteinn in *Gísla saga Súrssonar.* His assassin one night thrusts a spear through his chest as he is lying in bed. "Hneit þar" ("That hit"), Vésteinn says, and dies.

Now one must beware, of course, of drawing generalizations from instances like these. One has to do here with chief characters and heroes who have been endowed with no mean measure of courage and ambition. But their deportment, nevertheless, shows in what direction the ideal of a proud and dignified bearing lay. It is an ideal which strikes us as being singularly rigid and armor-plated. It has a certain affinity with the spirit and style of the ancient skaldic poetry, whose form made iron demands on the poet. One might say that the striving for human dignity and style has here been intensified and magnified to superhuman proportions. The strength of this ideal, where it occurs in its purest and most highly developed form, consists to a considerable degree in its one-sidedness. It is supported entirely by concern for one's personal honor and reputation.

Honor (Icelandic, *sómi, sæmð, virðing,* etc.) is ethically the key concept in the world of the Icelandic saga. This was not an abstract idea, but a deep and passionate experience, a condition of life as basic and essential as one's daily bread. But this need and desire for honor is expressed most strongly in the heroic figure. It stands out in especially sharp relief against the background of the sagas' pronounced fatalism. Even the greatest hero was unable to influence fate as such. What he did have control over was his own bearing and attitude toward fate, and this was determined ultimately by an intense feeling of what honor signified and demanded. If one fulfilled these demands, one could despite all else regard himself as master over his life and death. Here concern about one's posthumous fame is also involved. The honor a man has attained during life survives after death as his good repute. To a certain extent this good repute takes the place of personal immortality. A belief in the immortality of man does not exist in any form in the Icelandic sagas; they know nothing of feasting in Valhalla. The heroes of the sagas have the dictum of *Hávamál* about the "judgment of a dead man" engraved in their consciousness. In desperate situations they steel themselves with the need

99

and desire of achieving something that posterity will remember and talk about.

This easily wounded pride, this anxiously guarded honor is thus to a high degree socially conditioned. The people of the sagas are by no means unconcerned about what their fellow men think and say about them. Instances of individuals who defy public opinion are very uncommon. It might seem like an obvious conclusion to depict the figures of great outlaws as heroic misanthropes. But there is little evidence of such a self-sufficient individualism. The worth and honor of a human being are not a purely private matter. And a free man is not able to live without honor, or in any case to live as a respected fellow countryman.

The people of the sagas must always be on the alert, ready at all times to fight to preserve their honor. The ancient Icelandic language contains a wealth of expressions not only for the concept honor but also for disgrace and slander of various kinds. The sagas are just full of more or less venomous invective, not least of all in the form of accusations of unmanliness and similar charges. But each opprobrious word of that kind implies that the honor of the attacked person has been somewhat frayed at the edges. If he tacitly permits such slander to continue, the result may be fraught with dire consequences. The individual could not, in the long run, passively permit insult to be inflicted on him without eventually being regarded as a person of inferior worth. And this was of concern not only to him as an individual. As the member of a family, he thereby also jeopardized the honor and reputation of all his kinsmen, those of the living generation as well as those of past and future generations. Honor was a precious and irreplaceable possession which was not to be squandered and on which everything depended which made life worth living.

Under such circumstances the susceptibility to various forms of affront or insult must have become extremely intensified. Although they were quite conscious of the riskiness in this matter, many saga people seem to have had difficulty in suppressing the urge to make abusive and sarcastic comments. Consequently there were many opportunities for people to have their feelings hurt and to demand suitable retribution. The instances are legion in the sagas of how vehemently one could react under such circumstances, perhaps more violently than to many more obvious transgressions against life and property.

In *Njála* we read that Hallgerðr scornfully refers to Njáll as the beardless old man and to his sons as "dungbeardlings." In addition to that, she urges a certain man to compose some verses on the subject. And so he did, "and all of them were malicious verses," that is, they contained imputations of deficient manhood. Some roaming beggar women transmit this talk to the mistress at Bergþórshváll. She in turn passes on the information to her husband and their sons as they are sitting at table with the comment: "You have now received gifts, both father and sons, and it will be unmanly of you not to repay them." And she rounds off her chiding with still another rebuke, more direct than the previous one: "And if you do not take just vengeance for this, you will never avenge any disgrace." The men reply to her by trying to minimize the affront, but they cannot conceal their emotions:

"Our old mother takes great pleasure in teasing us," said Skarpheðinn with a grin. But sweat burst out on his forehead, and red spots appeared on his cheeks, and this was unusual. Grímr said nothing but bit his lips. Helgi's face remained impassive. (Chap. 44.)

On that very same evening, after the people on the farm have all gone to bed, the sons of Njáll set out and kill Sigmundr, the author of the malicious verses. "Good luck to the work of your hands," exclaims their peaceful father when they return and report what they have done.

Gunnarr of Hlíðarendi once received a scratch from a spur as a man galloped past him. At a banquet someone insinuates that Gunnarr had cried when Otkell rode over him and cut open his ear. The remark is reported by a herdsman to Gunnarr himself, who replies: "Let us not be distressed by words, but from now on you need do only such work as you care to." This mark of favor is, of course, an expression of Gunnarr's valuation of the herdsman's information. And he immediately prepares to wash off the disgrace. His halberd rings loudly when he grasps it. "Now you look so fierce, my son," says his mother. "I have never seen you like this before." The defamatory talk which is being noised about is in this case more fraught with dire consequences than the episode itself. Because it has become a general topic of conversation and is being interpreted as a sign of weakness on Gunnarr's part, it has become a matter of vital significance for his good name and reputation. It has become a matter of honor for him to take vengeance. The comment of the saga about Gunnarr's thorough retaliation is also characteristic: "Now people far about learned of this, and many said they did not think it had happened any sooner than was to be expected."

When honor and vengeance on behalf of a kinsman are at stake, the women of the sagas play a very prominent role. Bergþóra knows how to re-enact the disgraceful accusations against her husband and sons in such a way as to arouse them to the highest possible pitch of emotion. So, too, Guðrún in *Laxdæla* incites her brothers to make an attack on Kjartan:

> You would be endowed with fine dispositions if you were the daughters of some farmer or other, and did nothing either to help or to harm anyone. But after such shame and disgrace as Kjartan has done you, you lie there asleep even though he is riding past the house with only one companion. People such as you have the memory of a pig. (Chap. 48.)

A similar accusation of unmanliness occurs later in the saga when the mother of the slain Kjartan and her sons ride past Bolli's farmstead. She sighs deeply at the thought that Kjartan's killers are still alive, and says:

How different you have become from your distinguished kinsmen, since you are unwilling to avenge such a brother as Kjartan was. Your grandfather Egill would not have behaved that way. It is a hard thing to have sons who lack courage, and I truly believe you would be better fitted to be your father's daughters and to be given away in marriage. (Chap. 53.)

Sometimes the men try to resist the women's attempts to incite them to vengeance. Hildigunnr in *Njála*, "the sternest and harshest of women," resorts to drastic measures to goad her uncle Flosi into avenging her slain husband— or else her uncle should "be called the vilest of scoundrels." "You are a terrible monster," replies Flosi. "You would have us do something that would have the worst consequences for all of us. Cruel, indeed, is the counsel of women." He was so agitated that "his face was as red as blood, then as pale as grass, and then as black as Hel."[1]

One can understand the reactions of Hildigunnr as well as those of Flosi against the background of the ideology of the sagas. In spite of people's unexampled sensitivity in all matters pertaining to honor, the more considerate ones sometimes experienced a feeling of opposition and resistance to the unconditional fulfillment of the demands of honor. For in most cases these demands implied blood vengeance, which, carried out to its logical conclusion, with slaying upon slaying, could lead eventually to the annihilation of one's own family. To be sure, it was regarded as honorable for a man to expose himself to danger. Those who tried to protect their reputations merely by everywhere anxiously remaining in the background failed to gain the esteem of others as long as they lived. On the other hand, no one was obligated constantly to rattle his weapons and to defy death. Professional trouble-makers such as berserkers and other men of violence are never the favorite characters of a saga. The true hero well knows what he is risking, and therefore does not act recklessly. One of the most obviously idealized figures of saga literature, Gunnarr of Hlíðarendi, says on a certain occasion: "I do not know whether I am less courageous than other men because I find it harder to kill men than others do." One might perhaps be tempted to find in Gunnarr's confession a trace of the influence of the milder spirit of Christianity; this spirit is revealed in other ways in *Njála*. But even such a work as *Heiðarvíga saga*, which is of a type that belongs in every respect to a definitely earlier period, bears witness to the fact that sheer foolhardiness was not counted among the heroic virtues. Barði, the chief person in the story, delays the vengeance which he is obligated to exact, and thus exposes himself to relentless goading from everyone in his immediate surroundings. After very carefully laying the plans for his undertaking, he finally does take vengeance, but in such a moderate way that it arouses the vociferous displeasure of his supporters.

But such incitement from relatives or others who were close to the injured party need not in principle be regarded as irresponsible. It served a deep and serious purpose by keeping open the wound of disgrace. If this were permitted to heal unavenged, it could in time form a kind of lingering poison in the body of the family and destroy its vital force from within. To take revenge for inflicted losses or attacks, to vindicate one's honor, became a peremptory, unconditional command. When Þorgeirr in *Fóstbræðra saga* has fulfilled the requirement of blood vengeance for the death of his father by slaying the latter's killer, his mother exclaims: "Now you have accomplished that which was most necessary."

Nothing is said about the duty of vengeance in the ancient laws of Iceland. The concept of revenge had its roots in a deeper, more non-rational layer of consciousness than that to which the legal statutes appealed. But one must

104

not infer that this concept found expression in a completely arbitrary manner. On the contrary, vengeance was regulated by very definite principles. The point of departure was the integrity of the family. It was necessary to inflict damage upon the family of one's opponent which was at least as great as the injury one's own family had suffered. One of the most difficult situations one could get into, therefore, was to have to deal with an enemy who was too insignificant to give one complete satisfaction. If a free man were injured or killed by a thrall, vengeance exacted on the perpetrator of the deed did not signify any real redress. It was with this feeling that Ingólfr, for example, in *Landnámabók* stood before the body of his sworn-brother Hjörleifr, who had been killed by thralls: "What a distressing end for an honorable man, to be slain by thralls." With this comment he does not intend to say anything evil about thralls as such. They merely were regarded as belonging to a different category from that of free men. They had no share in his concept of fame and honor and consequently could not be included in the prevailing code of vengeance. But even where free men were concerned, the individuals' "rate of exchange" in the calculations of revenge varied considerably. If the person who committed the offense was insignificant, one usually preferred to direct the act of reprisal against a more highly regarded member of his family. The slaying of a distinguished and prominent man, on the other hand, might require several killings as adequate requital. But since the contending parties naturally evaluated somewhat differently, there was a risk that the reciprocal exacting of vengeance might degenerate into an endless feud. Yet it was not a question of purposeless bloodshed, nor did useless killing meet with general favor. On the contrary, it was regarded as a threat to order and security in the community. It was also customary for men who enjoyed the confidence of both parties to bring their influence to bear for the purpose of bringing about arbitration. If their efforts were successful, their own reputation was enhanced.

Honor, moreover, also had other aspects for the people of the sagas besides that which looked toward injury and revenge. One might mention as an example the custom of sworn brotherhood or, more generally, the loyalty between individuals who stick together in a common cause. In such cases the affinity not infrequently lasts until death. This faithful adherence of two persons to each other has found almost proverbial expression in the form of the declaration: "Now one and the same fate shall befall us both," which is sometimes uttered in situations where one or the other person might have the possibility of escaping alive. When Bergþóra is urged by Flosi, the leader of the incendiaries, to leave the burning house, she replies: "I was young when I was married to Njáll, and I promised him then that one and the same fate should befall us both." The pathos of the situation is further intensified when the little boy Þórðr refuses to leave his grandparents. Njáll and Bergþóra place him between them in their bed, where they await death.

To shelter a man in one's home implied unconditional obligations. If one received a man in distress, this was tantamount to a binding promise to aid him. The sagas contain ample evidence of the fact that even very insignificant persons gave protection to fugitives from their pursuers, even if this entailed the risk of incurring the wrath of a powerful chieftain. In a case like that the demands of honor and propriety could even supersede those of family loyalty. In one of the lesser sagas a man happened to grant hospitality to the murderer of a kinsman of his while still unaware of his guest's identity. But even after he had a clear idea of how matters stood, he continued to protect his guest even from his own relatives. When he was later called to account for his conduct he merely replied: "It seemed to me to be the only fitting thing to do."

The whole disposition toward violence, which in the eyes of the modern reader seems to characterize saga literature to a considerable degree, is regulated at least theoretically by an ideology which is founded on the concept of honor. There is no doubt that candor in one's dealings with all people, even with one's enemies, was regarded as an ideal virtue. When old Kveld-Úlfr in *Egils saga* tries to avoid taking sides for or against Haraldr hárfagri, his son Þórólfr disapproves of such an attitude: "Now I regard it as most unseemly to be neither his friend nor his enemy." Lack of clarity in such matters was generally looked upon with distrust or distaste. On one occasion Egill Skalla-Grímsson with his vikings made a coastal raid and during the night made off with much booty plundered from a farm. As they are making ready to put to sea again, Egill begins to think the matter over: "We have robbed this farmer of his goods and he does not even know it. Such a disgrace must not remain clinging to us." Thereupon he turns back all by himself and sets fire to the farmhouse!

To slay someone was regarded as dishonorable murder only if the manslaughter was not immediately made public according to the dictates of the law or if it was committed under cover of the dark of night—*náttvíg eru morðvíg*, "manslaughter during the night is murder." Clearly it was generally regarded as obligatory to wake a sleeping adversary before one made an attack upon him. But in actual practice this was often scarcely more than an empty gesture. In *Fóstbrœðra saga*, for instance, we read that Þorgeirr "went up to Gautr's bed and wakened him. Gautr sprang up and wanted to seize his weapons—but at that very moment Þorgeirr hewed at him and split his head down to the shoulders." The intended victim was thus given not the slightest chance to put up a real defense.

To use cunning or guile against an enemy was not regarded as disgraceful for a warrior or hero. Even such an idealized figure as Gunnarr of Hlíðarendi went about disguised as a merchant in order to trick an opponent. Gísli Súrsson escaped his pursuers on one occasion by successfully playing the role of a well-known idiot. Víga-Glúmr swore ambiguous oaths; and Guðrún Ósvífrsdóttir, proud as she was, at the instigation of sly Snorri goði, chose her words in such a crafty way that she was able to wriggle out of a given promise. Taken as a whole, the sagas yield many examples of petty slyness and cunning which are difficult to harmonize with the intense and delicate sense of honor which otherwise determines the style of life of the saga characters. Especially when vengeance is involved, one shrinks back at nothing. The compulsion to exact vengeance can justify even a deed which in itself would otherwise be dishonorable. Assaults from ambush and attacks with overwhelming odds are not unusual. Even hired assassins, so-called *flugumenn*, are not completely lacking.

One would distort the picture of the world of the sagas if one were to pass over such features in silence. But in this connection one must not forget that the social order of that day afforded the individual only a very weak protection of his rights. In every respect the individual must have lived in a condition of personal insecurity which is incomprehensible for us today. In such an era of blood-vengeance and lurking danger to life, one could well be tempted to resort to measures which were not overly punctilious. But even if the ideal demands of honor thus appear to have enjoyed only limited validity in the everyday life of the sagas, they were nevertheless present as a background or undercurrent. For this reason these sagas, despite all their ruthless realism, never give the reader a revolting feeling as *Sturlunga* sometimes can do with its authentic descriptions of base and senseless cruelty. The narratives dealing with the Saga Age are on a loftier plane and are enveloped by a purer atmosphere. They are probably not so much a true picture of historical reality as they are a creation of their authors' longing and idealization.

The pagan mode of thought is so distinctively characteristic of the sagas that traces of a more modern way of thinking stand out in sharp contrast. Such signs of foreign influence are found rather frequently, not least of all in several of the more significant works such as *Laxdæla* and *Njála*. These represent primarily reflections of Christian principles and values. Christianity, it will be remembered, became the official religion of Iceland during the Saga Age itself. And when the sagas were written during the thirteenth century, the country had been Christian for over two hundred years. It would have been nothing short of miraculous if Christianity had not left its mark in this literature.

The leading feminine character in *Laxdæla*, Guðrún Ósvífrsdóttir, had a completely pagan disposition. But in her old age she became "a very pious woman," the first in Iceland who "learned the psalms." She spent the last days of her stormy life, which included four marriages, as "the first nun and hermitess of Iceland." The foster brothers Kjartan and Bolli were early baptized in Norway. From this time on Kjartan is said to have "fasted on dry food throughout Lent, and he did this without the example of anyone here in this country; for people say that he was the first man to fast this way in Iceland. This seemed such an extraordinary thing that Kjartan should live so long without ordinary food that people came long distances to see him."[2] The author of the saga has thus made two chief characters into models in the observance of Christian practice. This might indicate that he himself was a man of the church. But the influence of Christianity in the case of Kjartan is shown not only in the superficial execution of religious rites but also in his behavior and actions. When Bolli draws his sword to slay Kjartan, the latter says: "It is a shameful thing you are about to do, kinsman; but I think it much better to be killed by you, kinsman, than to kill you." Thereupon he threw down his weapons and received the deathblow.

This dramatic scene was witnessed by a farmer named Þorkell, who afterwards spoke sneeringly about it; he called

Kjartan an effeminate and fainthearted man and often mimicked his behavior as he awaited the finishing blow. One of Kjartan's brothers had Þorkell seized in his house, led outside, and put to death; the farmer, the saga says, behaved "unmanfully" in the face of death. The author obviously regarded this low-minded fellow with aversion and contempt. And yet, it is really Þorkell who represents the older and genuinely pagan point of view. Kjartan's gesture, influenced by the Christian ideals of chivalry, created in the eyes of this simple farmer the impression of being overwrought and affected. Here was lacking the unyielding self-defense and proud self-vindication to the very end which characterized the more original Norse heroic ideal.

Njáls saga offers a rich variety in its portrayal of people, running the entire gamut from completely pagan to truly Christian. Of the chief characters, Hallgerðr and Skarpheðinn seem to lack the slightest trace of Christian virtues. Skarpheðinn's nature finds expression not least of all in his constant sardonic sneering and in his laconic utterances and retorts which are ironic to the utmost degree. His concluding performance, before succumbing in the flames, was to take from his belt-pouch a jaw tooth, which on an earlier occasion he had struck from the mouth of an enemy, and hurl it into the eye of one of his attackers so that the eye hung down on his cheek.

An incredible combination of pagan desire for revenge and Christian idiom is found in Hildigunnr's attempt to incite her uncle Flosi to vengeance for her husband Höskuldr:

> I call to witness God and all good men, and I implore you by the miracles of your Christ and by your own manliness and valor that you avenge every wound he had on his body when he was slain, or else may you be called the vilest of scoundrels. (Chap. 106.)

Hildigunnr, to be sure, was an exceptionally proud and stern woman. But that the sense of honor and vengeance in the pagan sense remained tenaciously alive even in people who otherwise appear to have been influenced decisively by Christian principles is shown by the example of Njáll himself. While the fire is raging he calms the women of the household with these words: "This will be only a little storm, and there will not soon be another one. Have faith in God's mercy. He will not let us burn both in this world and the next." And after commending his soul to God, Njáll quietly awaits death. Yet when Flosi a short time before offered to let him leave the burning house unharmed, he replied: "I will not go out, for I am an old man and scarcely able to avenge my sons; but I am not willing to live in shame." As already pointed out, Njáll also greets with a feeling of relief and satisfaction the news of his sons' swift vengeance exacted for the calumny directed against them and himself.

The most paradoxical combination of heathen mentality and Christian profession is afforded by one of the secondary characters of the saga, the blind Ámundi, the son of Njáll's natural son Höskuldr. Through a miracle he is enabled to see for a few moments, just long enough to wreak vengeance on the slayer of his father. "Praise be to Thee, Lord God. Now I see what Thou wilt," he exclaims as his eyes are opened. He leaps across the room to his surprised adversary and drives his axe up to the hilt into his head.

In connection with a serious legal dispute one of the chieftains in *Njála*, Hallr from Síða, renounces all redress for his slain son merely for the purpose of facilitating a general arbitration among the litigants. He says he is willing to show himself once more as a *litilmenni*. This word—a compound of *lítill* ("little") and of a derivation of *maðr* ("man")—was applied to a person who had but little concern for his own reputation and dignity. Within the pagan scale of concepts it therefore had a humiliating and degrading

111

connotation; its antonym, which had strongly positive implications, was *mikilmenni*, the first element of which is *mikill* ("great"). When a prominent chieftain can designate himself as a *lítilmenni*, it is evident that a revision of the scale of values has taken place under the influence of the Christian ideal of humility.

Höskuldr Hvítanesgoði, the foster brother of Njáll's sons, is probably the character in this saga who appears to be most strongly permeated by the spirit of Christianity. He does not exact vengeance for the slaying of his father, and remains impervious to the incitement of friends and kinsmen. He once declares that he would rather lie unatoned himself than to have many persons suffer on his account. But according to the older way of thinking, a man could scarcely suffer a more distressing fate than to be slain and then remain unavenged. One reason for looking up to Grettir the Strong as an ideal was that "he was avenged abroad in Miklagarðr (Constantinople), the only Icelander ever to be avenged there." But when Höskuldr falls before his attackers, he utters only these words: "May God help me and forgive you." This entreaty for forgiveness for his killers is reminiscent of the words of Jesus on the Cross. In the description of the saga Höskuldr also stands out as an innocent sacrifice, a martyr to human malevolence and to his own peaceful ideals. He goes out to sow grain in an enclosed field, while those who have plotted his death are hiding behind the enclosure. It is not often that the sagas describe nature and the state of the weather unless they have a direct bearing on the action of the story. But on the morning on which Höskuldr is slain, it is especially stressed that the weather was good and the sun was shining. The entire situation of the peaceful sowing of grain in the early morning affords a touching contrast to the blackness of the atrocious deed. It is as though the very light of day were concentrated into a resplendent nimbus about the figure of Höskuldr.

Christian influence is thus revealed in many ways and in many places in the sagas, ranging from the superficial to the more profound. This, of course, was to be expected. What is truly remarkable, however, is that this literature, taken as a whole, should have remained so singularly unaffected by Christian norms. One might perhaps be tempted to suspect in this the result of an extraordinarily faithful and tenacious tradition from the saga age. The ideology of the older pagan era and its models of heroic behavior would thus be somewhat like fossil remains which had survived practically intact throughout several centuries of Christianity. But actually it is scarcely necessary to resort to that kind of explanation.

Judging from the contemporary document *Sturlunga,* the leaven of the new religion, even in the twelfth and thirteenth centuries, had scarcely permeated the habitual manner of thinking of the Icelanders. The ancient scale of values, rooted in the concepts of honor, self-assertion, and vengeance, appears still to have been very much alive. In a verse which was composed in the year 1222 following a punitive expedition against Bishop Guðmundr we read the following: "Proud Sturla has exacted fitting vengeance for Tumi—the raven is standing on the corpse: Christ rules over glory and safety." The Prince of Peace has been assigned a place in the ideology of the blood-feud, and has been made to take over the old war-god Óðinn's bird, the black guardian spirit of the battlefield.[3]

CHAPTER 9

Humor and Irony

IT FOLLOWS AS a matter of course that humor or comedy as a chief motif can occur but rarely in the Sagas of Icelanders; tragedy occupies too large a place for that in this hero-extolling literature. Actually, if we disregard certain of the *þættir*, it is possible to name only one real exception: *Bandamanna saga*, i.e., the story of the confederates.[1] A whole gang of chieftains conspire together to cut short the career of an enterprising young man. With the weight of their combined strength they plot to have a judgment pronounced against him at the General Assembly depriving him of all of his possessions, which they intend to divide as spoils among themselves. The young man, Oddr, is completely baffled by their intrigue. But his old father Ófeigr succeeds with the aid of liberal bribes in bringing the conspiracy to nought by getting several of the chieftains to deceive their colleagues at the critical moment, so that the conspiracy turns into a fiasco at the General Assembly. The author fairly delights in exposing the avariciousness of the wealthy farmers; and in the scene at the General Assembly Ófeigr does a thorough job of nailing the conspirators fast to the pillory. On top of everything, the plotters get into a coarse wrangle among themselves. Here one can detect not the slightest breath of heroic idealism. Everything is on the petty scale of everyday life—depicted with a keen and sovereign eye for comical effect.

On the other hand, there are sagas which, practically speaking, seem to lack even the slightest touch of humor. To this type belong such well-known younger sagas as *Hrafnkels saga* and *Gunnlaugs saga ormstungu*, which otherwise are quite different from each other. But on the whole, almost every saga yields examples of one form or another of humor and irony. It is difficult to establish any definite difference between older and more recent sagas in this respect; the very difficulty of dating the sagas precisely precludes all possibility of certainty. Several of the famous later sagas, such as *Njála* and *Grettla*, are brimful of banter. But this also holds true for *Heiðarvíga saga*, which is often regarded as the oldest of the preserved sagas.

As a rule the humor of the Sagas of Icelanders tends toward irony and sarcasm. It often takes the form of austere understatement and laconic repartee in situations in which it is a matter of life and death. During the attack against Gunnarr at Hlíðarendi one of the attackers climbs up on top of the house in order to learn whether Gunnarr is at home. Through an opening in the roof he receives a halberd-thrust through the abdomen. He tumbles down from the roof and staggers back to his companions, who are sitting on the ground waiting for him. "Is Gunnarr at home?" someone asks. "That you will have to find out yourself," replies Þorgrímr, "but one thing I do know: his halberd was at home." Thereupon he falls down dead. In *Droplaugarsona saga* one of the chief characters has his lower lip cut away by a sword stroke. His comment to his opponent is: "My face never was handsome, and you have done little to improve it." Then he stuffs his beard into his mouth and holds it fast with his teeth as he continues to fight.[2]

The sagas also yield samples, although more parsimoniously, of a form of humor which is not directly connected with vengeance and armed conflict, and which can induce harmless laughter. About Gísli Súrsson's thrall Þórðr, for instance, the author says: "His intelligence was quite equal to his courage, for he possessed not a trace of either one." A similar comical formulation made as a sort of offhand remark is found in the same saga in a passage dealing with a farmer called Refr and his wife. The author tells us that Refr was extremely cunning. He continues: "Refr was married to a woman named Álfdís, who was pretty to look at but was a most ill-natured and quarrelsome shrew. Refr and his wife were a perfect match." In these two instances it is the author who with his own individual manner of description lends the passages a humorous touch. Sometimes, however, the humor arises from the nature of the situation itself; and in such cases it is often pointed up by means of a soberly objective exchange of words. *Droplaugarsona saga* describes how the farmer Þorgrímr skinnhúfa is deserted by his wife in the middle of the night. She names witnesses, declares herself divorced from her husband, and leaves home with a relative who has come there for the purpose of assisting her in this matter. In order to be safe from pursuit, she throws all her husband's clothing into the toilet before leaving. Only after all the people have gone away does Þorgrímr, who obviously is not conceived of as a very great hero, go into action. He sprang out of bed

and took his bed-cover and wrapped it around himself, for he had no clothing. He ran to the farm called Hof. Here lived Þórarinn moldoxi, who was a man of some importance.

Þórarinn said, "Why have you come here so early, Þorgrímr, and so lightly dressed?"

He replied and said that his wife had been taken away from him. "And now I want to ask your help in this matter."

Þórarinn said, "First of all I must give you some clothing, for that is what you need most now."

Later he ate his breakfast there. (Chap. 9.)

Through Þórarinn's reference to the clothing the reader is again reminded of the absurdity of the situation. This kind of soberly commonplace utterance is a comical contrast to the tragic ideal of heroism and vengeance which otherwise dominates the world of the sagas.

Hallfreðar saga tells about the love affair of the skald Hallfreðr with Kolfinna, the daughter of the farmer Ávaldi.

A steadier and more sober wooer for the hand of Kolfinna appears on the scene, however, in the person of a farmer named Gríss. With a number of backers he calls upon Ávaldi at his farm and gains from him his promise of his daughter's hand in marriage. While these negotiations are going on, Hallfreðr also makes his appearance. He finds Kolfinna there and immediately begins a very palpable flirtation with her. He sets her on his lap by the wall of the women's bower in plain view of all who come out. "He drew her close to him, and now and then there was some kissing." The saga continues:

> Now Gríss and the others came out. He said: "Who are those people sitting by the wall and acting so intimately?" Gríss was rather nearsighted and bleary-eyed.
>
> Ávaldi said: "That is Hallfreðr with my daughter Kolfinna."
>
> Gríss said: "Do they usually behave that way?"
>
> "It does happen often," said Ávaldi, "but now it is up to you to deal with this difficulty, for she is your future wife." (Chap. 4.)

Persons like Þorgrímr skinnhúfa and Gríss can be said to be comical characters *in nuce*. But the sagas also contain examples of more highly developed comical figures. To be sure, they do not play a major role in this literature, but serve primarily to create a contrast to the heroism of the central characters. Fear and cowardice in themselves were comical defects in a time which respected physical courage and accomplishment in the use of weapons. As a rule, too, it is thralls and other insignificant persons who represent this pitiful negation of the warrior virtues. Nor is there any trace of sympathy for the chickenhearted; these are unmercifully exposed to ridicule. A notable exception, however, is found in *Njála*. Even in such a point this masterpiece of saga writing reveals its human richness, its wealth and diversity of character portrayal.

In the last part of the saga Kári towers high above the forces and people around him like a bright, shining hero, perhaps somewhat too resplendent, too idealized. Kári, the brother-in-law of the slain sons of Njáll, has managed to escape death in the flames at Bergþórshváll, and now is confronted with the task of avenging the dead. But he has little support in the district and therefore falls back for help and shelter upon an insignificant farmer, Björn of Mörk, whom he also asks to accompany him on his journeys of reconnoitering. He flatters Björn by calling him "keen-sighted and quick of foot," and says he thinks he would also be a "good man in a skirmish" in case there should be one. Björn is not slow in affirming and amplifying this, and predicts that his manliness will stand the hero in good stead. The saga continues:

His wife heard this and said: "The trolls take your bragging and blustering. You should not talk yourself and Kári into believing such nonsense. I will gladly give him food and everything else which I know will aid him. But, Kári, do not rely on Björn's hardiness, for I fear that this will not turn out to be as great as he pretends.

Björn replied, "You have often reproached me like this, but I am certain that I would not show my heels to anyone. And the fact of the matter is that few people assail me because there is no one who dares to. (Chap. 148.)

From the very outset, of course, the reader realizes that Björn's courageous declarations are not completely warranted. The real warriors of the sagas also permit themselves to indulge in ostentatious speech, but even Björn's choice of words arouses suspicion. They strike one as naive or, so to speak, as amateurish. One feels more inclined to place confidence in the judgment of his wife. Kári himself is well aware of what sort of fellow his companion is. In spite of his dangerous situation he cannot deny himself the pleasure of leading Björn on to further boasting and to getting him to brag about his knowledge of the tactics of fighting with weapons. Thanks to Kári's own valiant efforts at crucial moments, Björn is spared from being put to a really severe test, and he acquits himself quite respectably during his stint as weapon-bearer. Success, to be sure, somewhat tones down his bragging; but when he thinks of his wife, he becomes thoughtful. It is obvious to him that she would not believe a single word of his own report about his exploits, and therefore he asks Kári to place his assistance and cooperation in as favorable a light as possible when they meet her again. Kári is good-natured enough to tell Björn's wife that her husband had risen to the occasion and acquitted himself well, and thus peace within the household is preserved. In this episode about Björn from Mörk we find ourselves in an atmosphere quite different from the heroic mood which is characteristic of the classical sagas. Björn is not simply ridiculous, not merely the butt of sarcasm. Both Kári and the author of the saga see him in a conciliatory light; they do not begrudge him the little feather in his hat. Here one can truly speak of the dual aspect and function of humor, of its indulgent view of human frailties.

The basic theme in a classical Icelandic saga, certainly, is almost never conceived of in the spirit of humor or comedy. Yet the various forms of humor, irony, and sarcasm need not for this reason always occur merely as scattered specks of color. They can skillfully be fitted into the structural pattern of the saga, and can twine about the main action of the story in such a way as to accompany and to intensify it. As an illustration of this technique one might choose *Heiðarvíga saga* ("The Story of the Heath Killings").

Upon Barði, a somewhat phlegmatic and dilatory young man, rests the moral obligation of avenging a slain brother. But he has delayed doing so for a long time, and is therefore regarded with critical eyes by all the people around him. One day his serving men are returning home from mowing in the hayfields. One of them, who answers to the surname *melrakki* ("arctic fox"), comes walking by, dragging his scythe behind him on the ground. Barði says in jest: "Now the fox is dragging his tail behind him." But the farm hand is not slow in repaying him in kind: "It is true that I am dragging my tail behind me, and I am not lifting it up very high, if at all. But I have a feeling that you will drag your tail for a long, long time before you avenge the death of your brother Hallr." This stinging retort shows how keen the desire for revenge is among all the people in Barði's vicinity; even his serving men are depressed because retribution is so slow in coming. The saga states that Barði did not reprimand the man with a single word just then. But later in the day, when he is giving the same servant some work instructions, which, moreover, are connected with the approaching expedition of vengeance, he adds: "The work is difficult, but if you have not finished it within the time set, you will find out which one of us will carry his tail higher thereafter." Barði's own jest about the fox's tail turned out to be a boomerang. The serving man's rejoinder struck him in a tender spot; his own play on words was returned to him as a smarting admonition to exact vengeance.

But the goading subsequently assumes significantly more powerful forms of expression. During a meal, old Mother Þuríðr serves each of her three sons, including Barði, a huge chunk of the shoulder of an ox. In reply to a sarcastic and irritated remark about the unwieldy morsels, she retorts that their brother Hallr was cut into still larger pieces and that this did not seem important enough to his brothers to elicit any comment from them. She goes even further. In addition to the generous portions of meat she gives each of them a stone: her sons, she hints, have swallowed worse things than stones because they have still not dared take vengeance for their brother Hallr. There is a caustic sarcasm, a gruesome vividness in the symbolism of the mother, and the sons react violently to it. They push over the table with everything that is on it and rush out to their horses.

The saga describes how the old woman herself clambers up on a horse in order to accompany her sons on their expedition. "For I expect that then there will be less chance that certain daring deeds might not be carried out. And there will be no lack of goading, for that is what is needed." But, of course, the brothers do not want to have the enterprising and provoking old woman trailing along after them on their dangerous undertaking. When they come to a certain brook, Barði has one of his men servants loosen the girth of her saddle while pretending to fasten it. The old woman tumbles down head over heels into the water and then returns home, none the worse for her little adventure. Here an element of pure farce, a bit of comical relief, has been introduced into the narrative before the central action of the story begins.

Before completing his dangerous mission, Barði receives a final upbraiding from his foster father, who sets up a detailed plan for the execution of the expedition of vengeance. He also quotes for Barði the derisive question which has come to be a common saying among his opponents in the Borgarfjörður District: "Don't you think Barði will come?" Nothing is said about Barði's reaction to the scorn in this phrase, but one can imagine that it sits like a thorn in the mind of the seemingly unperturbed man as he rides along.

As the story continues, the phrase about Barði's coming recurs again and again with increasing intensity and with ever deeper significance. One of his enemies—they are busy cutting hay on a meadow—thinks he can distinguish Barði among some men in the distance. But Gísli, the chief object of Barði's vengeance, goes on mowing and says to his

121

two brothers: "You have been acting all summer long as though you expected Barði to jump up from behind every bush, but he still hasn't come." The tragic irony here lies in the fact that it is Barði's intended victim himself who is mistaken: this time Barði really has come. Directly after Gísli's retort the situation becomes perfectly clear; his brother Ketill remarks: "Perhaps it won't turn out to be false that Barði really has come." The brothers try to reach their weapons, but they cannot get to them before their enemies are upon them.

Gísli is cut down by Barði not far from the house, and Ketill hastens away, carrying his brother's body on his back. Their father, who is at home working in the forge, knows nothing of what has happened. He is waiting for the return of a servant whom he has sent for some wrought iron. When he now hears someone walking outside, he unsuspectingly resorts to the usual jest, the current popular phrase of the family: "There's certainly a lot of noise. Has Barði still not come?" At that very moment Ketill steps into the forge with the answer on his lips: "Your son Gísli found out that he has come,"—and casts the dead brother down before his father's feet.

Purely from the standpoint of structure and composition, humor and irony are utilized very skillfully in the description of Barði's vengeance. It begins with his own pun about the fox's tail. But even this jest, which appears so innocent on the surface, soon turns out to be virulent. Then follows Mother Þuríðr's crude goading with the ox shoulder and the stones. Her own attempt to assist in the mission of vengeance meanwhile ends up as a farcical scene. Finally comes the contribution of the foster father in the form of his reference to the derisive question: "I wonder if Barði isn't coming?" From here on, this question with an increasingly suggestive effect accompanies the course of the action up to its culmination. Only against the background of the deep earnestness of the described events does the humor of this saga attain its full impact and effectiveness. And this is intimately connected with the whole view of life as portrayed in the sagas.

CHAPTER 10

Several Individual Sagas

THE ICELANDIC SAGAS of native heroes comprise a rather extensive literature. In a complete edition (*Íslendinga sögur* [Reykjavík, 1946–1949]) they fill twelve volumes. Even if one excludes certain late efforts in the saga style which have been printed in this edition, there remain eleven volumes of from four hundred and fifty to five hundred pages each. There are, to be sure, a large number of *novella* pieces, so-called *þættir*, "strands," included. The works which are designated as sagas—in all about forty—are of greatly varying length. The most voluminous is *Njála*, which is over four hundred pages long, followed closely by *Egils saga Skallagrímssonar* and *Grettis saga* with over three hundred pages each. The shortest sagas, on the other hand, may run to only ten to twenty pages.

It has long been customary to group the various Sagas of Icelanders according to the Icelandic districts in which the stories take place. Thus, for example, the edition just mentioned contains a volume called *Borgfirðinga sögur*, another called *Vestfirðinga sögur*, a third named *Austfirðinga sögur*, etc. The reason for this classification is supported especially by the fact that the actual landscape and settlements of Iceland play an essential role in the sagas. There is generally a profusion of authentic place names and concrete topographical details in them. It is this feature which has strongly contributed to the firm belief in the sagas' historical reliability. But in reality this proves no more than that the author of a saga himself may have been intimately acquainted with the region in which he has placed the action of his story. Still another support for the regional classification of the sagas is to be found in the fact that one probably has to reckon with certain "schools" of saga writing which were connected with cultural centers in various parts of the country.

In spite of the rather homogeneous character of the sagas taken as a whole—at least when viewed from a distance—one can also discern significant differences in regard to choice of motive, trend of thought and feeling, spirit and general tone; and one can thus try to group the sagas according to these internal, literary criteria. As a complement to the foregoing general discussion of the sagas, with emphasis on their style, character portrayal, and view of life, a short descriptive account of the characteristic features of several of the more important works will be given.

In *Egils saga Skallagrimssonar,* for short called *Eigla,* Norway is the scene óf action for quite some time at the beginning of the story. Haraldr hárfagri has begun his undertaking to crush the provincial kings and concentrate all power in his own hands. The chief interest of this part of the story revolves about Haraldr's quarrel with Kveld-Úlfr and the latter's sons Þórólfr and Skalla-Grímr. Þórólfr, to be sure, quickly gains the confidence of the king and is entrusted with responsible commissions in his service. But he becomes the victim of insidious slander spread about in the king's retinue by men envious of him. Finally he is attacked on his own estate by the king himself with an overwhelming force and is there slain. This completes the rupture between the clan of Kveld-Úlfr and Haraldr hárfagri. Kveld-Úlfr and Skalla-Grímr have no other choice but to emigrate in order to escape the wrath of the king. Before they turn their keels toward Iceland, they succeed in giving the king a fitting souvenir as vengeance for Þórólfr: they come upon one of Haraldr's ships and execute a thorough blood-bath among the crew. Kveld-Úlfr dies on the voyage to the new land.

The situation in Norway as delineated here is, it will be seen, the one which has traditionally been regarded as the cause of the large-scale colonization of Iceland. Many episodes in this section of the story are splendidly told. Just take, for example, the description of how the insidious slander of the sons of Hildiríð brings about the fall of Þórólfr. Memorable, too, is Skalla-Grímr's appearance before the king following the slaying of his brother. In the contrast between the two brothers, Þórólfr and Skalla-Grímr, one of the chief themes in the description of the family is touched on for the first time: Þórólfr represents the light and candid, Skalla-Grímr the dark and taciturn side.

The description of the settlement on the Borgarfjörður in the southwest of Iceland breathes the fresh atmosphere of discovery and pioneering. A virgin country is explored. There is good seal hunting and an abundance of fish everywhere. Very quickly the saga concentrates on Skalla-Grímr's son Egill. The precocious lad soon reveals his true nature: it is that of the skald and the warrior. At the age of three he composes his first verses, not without skillfully contrived kennings; at the age of seven he commits his first manslaughter against an eleven-year-old playmate. Egill belongs in many respects to that branch of his family which is dark and somber. He is a problem child who causes both his father and his more sober and steady brother Þórólfr much worry and trouble. In these two brothers, moreover, the contrast between their dead uncle Þórólfr and their father Skalla-Grímr is embodied anew.

In spite of grave doubts and reservations Þórólfr finally has to yield to his contentious, stubborn brother and take Egill along on a voyage to Norway. Such a trip abroad seems to have been part of the general education of sons of well-to-do farmers in Iceland. Egill's clan previously did not enjoy the best relations with the royal house in the land of their origin, where now Eiríkr blóðøx and his queen Gunnhildr are in power. Nor does the strong-willed young Icelander improve these relations; he succeeds, on the contrary, in making himself thoroughly impossible before these potentates. At a banquet, at which the royal couple are guests of honor, Egill drinks beer with a thirst which arouses justified amazement. The drinking suddenly comes to an end, however, when he thrusts a sword through the breast of the host. Egill escapes after an exciting flight.

Following this ostentatious exhibition Egill engages in plundering expeditions as a viking and has many adventures before finally settling down on his paternal estate, Borg. An event of great moment in Egill's life is the loss of his beloved brother Þórólfr in a large battle under the English king Aðalsteinn. Egill's continued controversy with the Norwegian royal couple runs like a red thread through the colorful course of his life. The queen especially stands out prominently as his bitter adversary, an extremely dangerous woman well-versed in witchcraft. Egill reacts with terrible vengeance to what he regards as his absolutely manifest rights—the matter concerns the inheritance of his brother's widow, whom he has now taken as his wife. Among other things, he kills one of the sons of the king and queen. On one of the outlying Norwegian skerries he erects a rune-inscribed *niðstöng,* "pole of insult," against King Eiríkr and Queen Gunnhildr, and accompanies the ceremony with powerful incantations in which he invokes the guardian spirits of the country to drive his royal enemies out of Norway. And whether or not this is caused by Egill's insult pole—within a short time Eiríkr and Gunnhildr have to go into exile.

Meanwhile Egill has not even had time to get word of this when, after a short time at home in Iceland, he is seized by an inexplainable restlessness and wanderlust. He makes ready a ship and sets out to find his former patron, King Aðalsteinn. He suffers shipwreck in a howling storm off the English coast without having the slightest idea that he has landed in the immediate vicinity of his mortal enemies Eiríkr and Gunnhildr. Egill now puts everything on one card. He seeks out his steadfast friend Arinbjörn, who is highly esteemed and trusted in the retinue of King Eiríkr, and in his company appears before the king and queen. Arinbjörn has to summon all of his high prestige in order to save his friend's life, at least until the next day. He urges Egill to use this respite of one night to compose an encomiastic poem about King Eiríkr. By the time dawn breaks, Egill has finished the poem; he recites it in the king's hall and as a reward for the poem he actually receives his own "wolf-gray head," as he says himself in a later poem in which he pays homage to his friend Arinbjörn. The poem recited in the presence of Eiríkr blóðøx thus had good reason to be named *Höfuðlausn* ("Head Ransom").

After this dramatic climax there follows a series of new colorful adventures in Norway and the neighboring province Värmland. Some of these episodes afford a good picture of the barbaric wildness in Egill's character. In a holmgang with a man who knows the art of "deafening" his enemy's sword, Egill hits upon the expedient of throwing himself over his opponent and biting his throat open. A farmer in Värmland, who in Egill's opinion was not sufficiently hospitable to him, gets his reward: early the next morning Egill breaks into the farmer's bed closet, draws his sword with one hand, seizes the farmer by the beard with the other, yanks him out on the bed-board, and cuts away the beard right down to the chin; "thereupon he crooked a finger in one of his eyes, so that it fell out on his cheek bone." That, declares Egill to the mother and daughter of the house, is a mild punishment for such a cur.

At times Egill can show himself from entirely different sides, such as when, through a successful duel, he saves a girl and her family from an ugly berserker and unwelcome wooer. On this occasion the churlish viking bears a certain resemblance to the knight who slays the dragon and frees the young maiden. A peaceful interlude is afforded by the description of how Egill with his superior insights into rune magic cures the daughter of a Värmland farmer of a long wasting illness.

Shortly after Egill's final return to Iceland, his favorite son Böðvarr is drowned. The father takes the loss very hard. After Böðvarr's body was placed in the ancestral burial mound, Egill takes to his bed, just as his grandfather Kveld-Úlfr did after the slaying of Þórólfr; he refuses to eat and drink and wishes only to die. His daughter Þorgerðr is summoned, the wife of the chieftain Óláfr pá and the mother of Kjartan in *Laxdæla*. With the help of an innocent subterfuge she succeeds in influencing the stubborn Egill to remain alive, at least long enough to finish a poem of commemoration for Böðvarr. This is a charming and vivid scene between father and daughter, in which his waning obstinacy is contrasted in an amusing and touching manner with her affection and psychological tact. According to the saga, therefore, we have Þorgerðr to thank for the fact that *Sonatorrek* ("The Terrible Loss of My Sons") was composed, a poem famous in the annals of Germanic literature.[1]

Hard it is to stir my tongue—thus begins the poem—and to draw forth song from the recesses of my soul. For sorrow oppresses: not happy is the man who bears his kinsman's corpse from his house. My kin has nearly come to an end, like a storm-lashed tree in the forest. Rán[2] has bereaved me of much. Could I take vengeance with my sword, then it would be the death of Ægir. But for this I have no strength; the old man's forlornness is clear as day. I have not been able to hold my head upright since the fever of sickness snatched away my other son.[3] Still do I remember when Óðinn took the support of my clan up to the abode of the gods.[4] I was on good terms with Óðinn and put my trust in him before the god of victory sundered our friendship. Reluctantly do I pay homage to him. Yet he has given me redress, a noble gift: the unfailing skill of poetry and a heart that turns false friends into frank foes. Now I am

.sad. Yet I will gladly wait for Hel, ungrudgingly and serene of heart.[5]

Sonatorrek (*ca.* 960) is generally regarded as the first great poetic expression in the North of the emotional life of an individual. Even today the poet's clearly individual traits of character stand out plainly to the reader: his bereavement and forlornness, but also his unbroken pride in being a poet. Almost every poem which Egill composed bears this personal stamp, a trait which is otherwise not so common in skaldic poetry.

The saga follows its chief character down to his last days, which Egill spent at Mosfell, the estate of his niece and stepdaughter Þórdís and her husband Grímr. Egill's hearing and eyesight fail him in his old age, and in the end he is completely blind. There is a striking contrast between the viking Egill at the height of his strength and the helpless old man who fumbles his way about, stumbling over his own feet, and ridiculed and scolded by the serving women. When in his eighties, he has a capricious whim. He takes it into his head to ride to the General Assembly with the two chests of English silver which King Aðalsteinn gave him. He intends to strew out from the Law Rock all of this silver among the throngs of people there in the hope of being able to enjoy the spectacle of the entire membership of the Assembly brawling and scuffling for the silver. Obviously he has been looking forward with childish pleasure to this battle royal during the boring existence of his old age. He takes his niece and stepdaughter Þórdís into his confidence in this matter, and she pretends to be sympathetic to his plan. She replies that it is a splendid idea, and that people will remember it and talk about it as long as the country is inhabited. But naturally the family takes steps to avert the old man's planned practical joke.

Eigla is one of the high points of saga literature. It is lucid and clearly constructed and—aside from the introductory part with Norway as the scene of action—concentrated to an unusual degree on the chief person. No other character in the sagas stands out in such monumental completeness of form, both physical and spiritual, as Egill. But Egill himself, through his poems, which were woven by the author into his narrative, has also made an extraordinary contribution to his own characterization.[6]

According to a rather old hypothesis Snorri Sturluson himself is believed to have written *Eigla*. This view was advanced by Grundtvig as early as the beginning of the nineteenth century. In recent years Sigurður Nordal, the foremost expert on both Snorri's authentic works and on *Eigla*, has adduced weighty evidence in support of it.[7]

Among other well-known sagas which resemble *Eigla* in having a poet as hero, one can mention *Hallfreðar saga* and *Kormáks saga*. In the latter, especially, the narrative is scarcely more than a connecting text between the main character's many *lausavísur* ("occasional verses") composed and recited in connection with various episodes in his life.[8]

In *Egils saga Skallagrímssonar* almost all interest is gradually concentrated on the title role. *Njála*, on the other hand, exhibits a whole series of figures of the first order, both men and women, and thus has a greater wealth of character portrayal. To be sure, the conventional voyages abroad and passages of arms are not lacking here. But in addition to this *Njála* also presents an unusually colorful and detailed picture of daily life in all its phases. Taken as a whole, no other classical saga possesses such human breadth as this one.[9]

Njáls saga, also called *Brennu-Njáls saga* (or *Njála* for short), can be divided into three major parts. The main action begins with the marriage of Gunnarr of Hlíðarendi and Hallgerðr. This is followed by a description of the friendship between Gunnarr and •Njáll and of the manner in which this friendship resists all stresses and strains to which it is subjected, especially through the machinations of Hallgerðr. This section culminates in the slaying of Gunnarr at his farm Hlíðarendi. In the next major portion Njáll and his sons come into the foreground. A major crisis in this part of the story is the slaying of Höskuldr Hvítanesgoði by the sons of Njáll. This evil deed leads to the climax of the entire saga, the burning of Njáll and his family in their home at Bergþórshváll. The third and final part describes at length and in great detail the litigation following the burning as well as the blood vengeance exacted by Njáll's son-in-law Kári. The drama concludes on a note of reconciliation. Both Flósi, the leader of the incendiaries, and his opponent Kári make pilgrimages to Rome in order to receive absolution from the pope himself. After the death of his wife, Kári takes to wife Flósi's niece Hildigunnr, who formerly incited her uncle so strongly to vengeance against Njáll's sons.

In the final section of the saga the course of events is sometimes interrupted by the insertion of material which is not especially closely related to the narrative as such.[10] Thus, for example, the account of how Christianity is introduced in Iceland is not in itself unmotivated, but it is related with such breadth of detail that it has been concluded that an independent description of this event was simply incorporated into *Njála* without much revision. Another insertion, the so-called Brján episode near the very end of the work, is thought to be derived from an older independent saga no longer extant; the scene of action of this episode is outside of Iceland and it is named for an Irish king. For modern readers the description of the legal proceedings following the burning of Njáll is far too voluminous. This long and detailed description seems to indicate that the author was especially interested in ancient laws and legislation.

Njála can be regarded as a decided tragedy of fate. Njáll himself endeavors to the best of his ability to reconcile the demands of honor with peace and good will among men. He knows that vengeance, as he himself once expresses it, sometimes can work this way and sometimes that way. Njáll himself is not completely lacking in imperiousness; and to achieve his ends he uses not only intelligence and authority, but also force and cunning. His intimate friend Gunnarr of Hlíðarendi and his foster son Höskuldr are perhaps the two men who best understand and appreciate his true nature and his ideals. Neither Njáll nor Höskuldr ever raises a weapon against a human being. And the warrior Gunnarr, who excels all of his countrymen in battle and athletic prowess, himself declares that he finds it harder to kill than other people do. But no matter how wisely Njáll lays his plans, he does not succeed in averting inexorable fate. The people in his immediate vicinity cannot deny their true violent natures in spite of their great veneration for him. And slander sows its dragon seed. When Skarpheðinn brings his father the news that Höskuldr has been killed, Njáll sees all his efforts to effect a reconciliation collapse; he predicts the death of himself, his wife, and his sons. After the slaying of Höskuldr it seems as though he has accepted fate. He no longer tries to influence events, but lets them run their course. Finally, during the fire itself, fate seems to be replaced in Njáll's thinking by providence. Beyond death fate has no power: "God is merciful. He will not let us burn both in this world and the next."

Fate directs the heavy stream of events in *Njála*. But within this framework the author gives artistic form to the psychological and moral problems with finer insight and finesse than any of his colleagues. This aspect of his art can be seen most clearly in the interaction among Njáll, his own sons, and his foster son Höskuldr. The sons of Njáll had little justification for killing Þráinn Sigfússon. Njáll sees to it that a composition of the case is brought about, and that full redress is made in the form of wergild. But afterward he takes a very noteworthy step: he offers to take Þráinn's young son Höskuldr as his foster son—such foster-

133

ing was always a gesture of friendship and esteem toward the child's real parents. Njáll's act is, as was said, extraordinary. For one of man's most sacred duties according to the old pagan concept of honor was to exact vengeance for the death of his father. And if the son happened to be still a child when his father was slain, then not only his friends and kinsmen but also public opinion absolutely demanded that the slain man be avenged as soon as the son was grown. No friendship, no deeds of kindness could soften the iron necessity of this inescapable duty.

With his offer to foster the slain Þráinn's son, Njáll thus takes up the battle against deeply rooted values. And it seems as though he would succeed. The bonds between him and his foster son grow to be very strong. Njáll imparts to Höskuldr a portion of his own view of life and of his own moral concepts, and the young man is uncommonly receptive to his teachings. Njáll's motives for taking Höskuldr as his foster son are very likely complex. This fostering is a manifestation of his celebrated wisdom, an attempt to efface guilt and thereby to avert a dreaded vengeance. But at the same time it bears witness to his good will, to his upright desire to make amends. In his relationship to Höskuldr the most beautiful elements of Njáll's character and of his view of life are crystallized. It is for this reason that he comes to love this spiritual son of his perhaps more than those who are his own flesh and blood.

It is a terrible blow to Njáll that his own sons permit themselves to be tricked into killing Höskuldr and thus committing an unheard of deed of infamy. "In truth, this grieves me so sorely that I would rather have lost two of my sons, if Höskuldr were still alive." When he says these words he is obviously thinking of the calamitous reaction which must follow such an evil deed; fate has mercilessly thwarted his wise forethought. But equally strongly his utterance gives spontaneous expression to his sorrow at the loss of his beloved foster son. It is as though his life sinew, his very will to live, collapses under this double strain. To this lament of Njáll, Skarpheðinn replies: "We must not be angry at your words. You are an old man, and it was to be expected that this would affect you deeply." It is quite conceivable that Njáll's sons felt somewhat hurt to learn that their own father did not esteem them as highly as he did his foster son. But it is also probable that they are somewhat baffled by the entire manner of thinking which finds expression in the relationship between their father and Höskuldr. In spite of the fact that from the very outset a strong friendship seems to prevail between the sons of Njáll and their foster brother, it appears somehow as though this friendship had a fragile foundation and was felt to be unnatural. If Höskuldr had had a different kind of temperament, i.e., the kind of temperament characteristic of most of the saga people, he would never have forgotten the slaying of his father but would have waited for an opportunity to exact blood vengeance from Skarpheðinn or from someone among his closest of kin. But Höskuldr, the person in the saga who impresses us as being most strongly permeated by the spirit and way of thinking of Christianity, has truly forgotten and forgiven; he does not brood about vengeance. And it is precisely this fact that the sons of Njáll cannot fully comprehend. Especially Skarpheðinn, Þráinn's killer, must be keenly conscious of what a great injury he has inflicted upon Höskuldr, and he probably never overcomes a certain feeling of uneasiness in his presence. When Mörðr Valgarðsson begins to sow distrust between Njáll's sons and their foster brother, Höskuldr proves to be completely immune. But with the sons of Njáll, Mörðr gradually gains ground. In his purposeful slander he cleverly works on the sense of guilt they feel toward their foster brother. To them it must seem quite reasonable, as Mörðr hints, that Höskuldr under his mask of friendship is getting ready to take vengeance. Finally the seeds of slander have ripened, the taunting of the sons of Njáll has reached its climax, and they decide to strike the first blow rather than to be struck by it. Through the slaying of a perfectly innocent man they bring about catastrophe for themselves and their kin.

Against the background of the glow of the fire from Bergþórshváll is enacted a drama of heroic proportions and great artistic power. It must have been created by a poet who, experienced in the ways of the world, had gazed deeply into the human heart and had pondered over its riddles in a spirit of serene freedom from illusion.

Laxdæla saga has already been cited as an example of the important role which dreams and fatalism play in the Icelandic sagas. But the unique charm of this story is to be found in the aura of romanticism and chivalric ideals which envelops its descriptions. The saga writer delights in dwelling on magnificent garments, riding gear, and weapons. After his return home from Miklagarðr, Bolli Bollason is said to have been so fond of splendor and display "that he did not want to wear any clothing except such as were made of scarlet and of silk wrought with golden thread, and all of his weapons were inlaid with gold." The picture of Bolli on horseback at the head of a train of attendants, all of them with scarlet garments and gilded saddles, is reminiscent of medieval manuscripts illuminated with clear, glowing colors:

> He was dressed in clothing made of silk wrought with gold, which the king of Miklagarðr had given him, and over this he had a scarlet cloak with a cowl. He was girded with the sword Fótbítr, of which the guard and boss were inlaid with gold and the hilt wound with gold. He wore a gilded helmet on his head, and at his side he carried a red shield adorned with a knight inlaid in gold. In his hand he held a lance of a kind then popular abroad, and wherever he and his followers took lodging, the women had no mind for anything else but to gaze at Bolli and at the finery of himself and his men. (Chap. 77.)

It is significant that in this saga the French loanwords *kurteiss* and *kurteisi* (from French *courtois* and *courtoisie*) are time and again applied to both Bolli and to other men. This is an epithet which would scarcely be suitable in a description of Egill Skalla-Grímsson or Skarpheðinn Njálsson.

A romantic episode in *Laxdæla* is the story of how the Irish princess Melkorka, who was abducted from her home by pirates, is bought by Höskuldr Dala-Kollsson from a Greek merchant on the Brenn Islands at the outlet of the Göta-elv and later becomes the mother of Óláfr pá and the paternal grandmother of Kjartan. In none of the other better-known sagas is so much space devoted to the women characters. The scene is dominated above all by Guðrún Ósvífrsdóttir. Indeed, she has come to stand as the archetype of the proud woman of pagan times whose violent emotions both in hate and in love demand their tribute of blood among the men in her life. "I was worst to him I loved the most," Guðrún confesses in her old age to her son Bolli. This is one of the classical quotations from the sagas, a paradoxically pointed formulation of tragic human experience.

But there are more spirited women than Guðrún in the gallery of characters in *Laxdæla*. One of these is Auðr, who goes about dressed in trousers like a man and who, sword in hand, personally takes revenge against her husband, who had himself divorced from her. Another is Þorgerðr, daughter of Egill-Skallagrímsson and mother of Kjartan. After Kjartan's death she reminds his brothers with burning sarcasm of the unatoned slaying. "It will not be your fault, Mother, if we should forget this," her son Halldórr assures her. When they make ready for the expedition of vengeance, she strongly insists on going along in spite of her sons' objections: "for I know my sons very well, and I know you need some egging on." When one of her sons during the assault on Bolli severs his opponent's head from his

137

body with a blow from his axe, the mother wishes him good luck to the work of his hands. Now, she adds triumphantly, Guðrún will be kept busy for a while combing out Bolli's curly red hair.

Women as instigators to vengeance figure prominently in saga literature. Nor will anyone deny that this phenomenon can have had a sound basis in reality. But it is obvious, on the other hand, that this motif was soon found to be a fruitful literary device and consequently was exploited to the utmost degree. Indeed, it sometimes assumes an irresistibly comical aspect, and this is certainly not unintentional. When Njáll's mistress Hróðný comes to Bergþórshváll with the dead body of her and Njáll's son Höskuldr, Bergþóra does not show in her behavior the faintest hint of jealousy, which under other circumstances would probably be a natural reaction to a visit by her rival. In the presence of Hróðný she turns to her own sons: "It is strange the way you behave. You slay men for little reason, yet about such a matter as this you stew and brood so that in the end nothing will come of it." This reprimand for being slow to take vengeance is undeniably somewhat surprising: Bergþóra's sons, waked in the middle of the night, have scarcely had time to rub the sleep out of their eyes!

How Mother Þuríðr in the archaic *Heidarviga saga* used drastic means to incite her sons to avenge the death of their brother has already been discussed (p. 120). This incident reminds us of the fact that this Þuríðr is the daughter of Þorgerðr in *Laxdæla,* who also was quite successful in taunting her sons. Some persons may perhaps think that the descriptions of mother and daughter in these two sagas substantiate the belief in the historical veracity of this literature: a daughter, after all, can be expected to reveal a way of thinking like that of her mother or to follow her example. But, on the other hand, it could also be tempting for a more freely creative author to establish just that sort of connection between the generations of the sagas. In any event, the descriptions in *Heiðarvíga saga* and *Laxdæla* of Þuríðr's and Þorgerðr's efforts to bring about vengeance resemble each other so strongly that one is inclined to suspect literary influence in one direction or another. The authors have merely developed the motif in different ways. In the more primitive *Heiðarvíga saga* it has been given a rustic-burlesque touch; in *Laxdæla*, which has a tendency toward courtly ideals and consequently little appreciation for austere irony and drastic humor, it has been treated in a more aristocratic spirit.

As a complement and contrast to the precocious warrior of the Egill Skalla-Grímsson type, the kind of hero who is very slow in his development stands out prominently in the sagas. He need not be lacking in intelligence; the stress lies, rather, on his indolence and his loafing around in the warmth of the kitchen. A youth of such a disposition is not the least concerned about the work on the farm. He prefers to lie stretched out full length by the fireplace in the kitchen and let people stumble over his feet; for this reason he is called a "coal-biter" or "fire-sitter." The "coal-biter" is regularly described as taciturn and unsocial. He likes to torment the people around him with more or less scurvy tricks. The chief character in *Grettis saga Asmundarsonar*, called *Grettla* for short, has been endowed with certain traits of this type. He certainly is not a folk-tale "ash-poker." But he develops slowly as a child, is quiet and reserved, but at the same time impudent and enterprising. He likes to compose verses, especially lampoons, and gives bitterly ironic answers. He sabotages in a hair-raising manner the only tasks his father entrusts him with.

The typical "coal-biter" in the sagas, much to the surprise of all who know him, usually takes a sudden farewell from his past and reveals an entirely new side of his nature. Sometimes the transformation is symbolized by the fact that

139

he simultaneously lays aside his childish or tattered clothing. No such metamorphosis takes place in the case of
Grettir. On the contrary, one gets the impression that the
author, through his description of Grettir's childhood,
wants to give an indication of his coming fate. Grettir, it
will be remembered, is famous above all as the great outlaw, the man who was able to live longer in outlawry than
anyone else in Iceland. But outlawry implies isolation and
loneliness. And Grettir appears lonesome even as a boy at
home, constantly on his guard against his father with sharp,
proverb-like retorts. The contrast between Grettir and his
older brother Atli is strongly underscored. The latter is
said to be "friendly and kind, gentle and mild-mannered,
and liked by everyone." He is prophesied a future as "an
energetic, prudent, and wealthy man," while Grettir's nature fills his father with premonitions of evil.

After this, the saga develops in a long series of fantastic
adventures, which give Grettir the opportunity to demonstrate his tremendous physical power. He battles successfully not only with ordinary berserkers but also against
ghosts and trolls. Especially dramatic is the description of
his nocturnal struggle against the fearful ghost Glámr. In
a manner which is extremely unusual in saga literature, a
description of nature is employed here to intensify the
mood of terror: "There was bright moonlight outside, and
heavy clouds with rifts in them. Sometimes the clouds
drifted over the moon, and sometimes the moon shone forth.
Now at the very moment in which Glámr fell, the clouds
drifted away, and Glámr stared piercingly up at Grettir.
And Grettir himself said that this was the only sight he had
ever seen which frightened him." (Chap. 35.) Before the
ghost is killed, he is able to put a terrible curse on his adversary: Grettir is to be condemned to outlawry, and he
will be compelled to live alone in the uninhabited waste-
land; he will also see Glámr's ghastly staring eyes before
him, and they will haunt him as long as he lives.

All these adventures viewed by themselves might appear to be a rather superficial kind of entertainment—apart from the fact that they are most skillfully related. But when they are seen in proper perspective in their relationship to Grettir, they seem to assume a special psychological and artistic significance. They emphasize the uniqueness and the wildness of the man himself and of his fate as an outlaw. The adventure with Glámr can even be interpreted as a symbolic verification of the fact that Grettir irrevocably is a man of great misfortune, as he is called time after time in the saga. Toward the end, however, the story assumes a more purely human and natural aspect. On the desolate cliff-island Drangey, his final place of refuge, the deathly-sick Grettir, fighting on his knees when he can no longer stand, is slain. And there the outlaw is not in ghostly loneliness. By his side stands his younger brother Illugi, who has faithfully shared the hardship of his last days on the island.

None of the other major sagas gives such striking prominence to the supernatural as *Grettla,* although witchcraft and hauntings are not lacking in several of them, especially in *Eyrbyggja saga.*[11] One might imagine that such motifs would contrast in an incongruous manner with the generally cool, objective tone of saga style. But, on the other hand, one must keep in mind the fact that these supernatural events in the eyes of the saga characters were a normal part of the world of reality. Furthermore the saga writers' extraordinary skill in narration does much to lend even the most fantastic episodes a certain suggestive realism. Grettir's intensely exciting struggle with the ghost Glámr, to cite just one example, is related practically blow by blow. The revenant is described so vividly and naturally that the reader is willing to accept his actual existence.

CHAPTER 11

The Decline of Saga Literature

ABOUT THE END of the thirteenth century the forces which produced the Icelandic sagas of native heroes seem to have been exhausted. The saga literature which still flourished bore a much less realistic stamp; most of these later works are therefore designated as *lygisögur*, "lying stories," of which there were various kinds.[1] This genre has been connected with the stream of international, romantic tales and poems which reached Iceland during the second half of the fourteenth century. Chivalric romances of the twelfth century—for example, the cycle of poems about King Arthur and his knights of the round table, together with other epics of Welsh or Breton origin—gradually spread over Europe. At the behest of King Hákon Hákonarson, a certain Friar Robert translated the famous love story of Tristan and Isolde into Norwegian in 1226.[2] With this translation the romance of chivalry—an expression of the courtly ideals of contemporary European nobility—was introduced into Norway, and a series of other translations followed.

It is quite probable that the Norwegian initiative influenced the Icelanders to undertake translations of a similar kind. But it is also possible that these translations played a certain role in the more independent authorship of the so-called *fornaldarsögur*. (See page 46 above.) The style of the heroic sagas is, at least superficially, very similar to that of the Sagas of Icelanders; the stories, in general, are constructed according to a similar plan and involve two or three generations. The tone is as objective as though the tales were authentic history; but their content is usually quite fantastic. The author has surrounded a hero such as Örvar-Oddr with all conceivable and many utterly preposterous adventures. Great deeds and exploits are piled up with a copious use of folk-tale motifs. The hero (Örvar-Oddr = Arrow-Oddr) was named for his arrows, which always returned to him after he shot them. He begins his heroic career by making a journey to Bjarmaland, where he performs marvelous deeds with a thick club in battles against the trolls. An Irish princess presents him with a magic shirt, which protects the wearer against cold, heat, all kinds of weapons, and even against starvation. It can fail to be effective only on one condition: if the wearer should flee from an enemy in battle—an eventuality which is completely unthinkable in the case of Örvar-Oddr! On one occasion he is abducted by a powerful griffin and given to her young for food in a crevice high up in the mountains which no ordinary human being can get in or out of. But of course Oddr, with the help of a giant, is able to escape even this situation, after which he continues his odyssey.[3]

Together with fantastic exploits and adventures, the love motif now becomes much more prominent than it was in the Sagas of Icelanders. As an example of this, one might mention the tale of Friðþjófr the Bold, which is especially well known, at least in name, thanks to the Swedish poetic version of the saga by Esaias Tegnér.[4]

One must not assume, however, that the chronological relationship between the Sagas of Icelanders and the *lygisögur* is altogether clear and distinct. On the one hand, there are indications that a style of writing of a highly fanciful and imaginative nature flourished side by side with the more sober and realistic sagas of native heroes. On the other hand, some of the later Sagas of Icelanders also reveal a certain amount of influence from foreign literature. But on the whole, the line of demarcation between the two ypes of sagas is quite clear; the difference between them is ot merely one of degree but also of kind.

At a rather early date prose literature encounters cometition which eventually proves to be overpowering. Around the turn of the fourteenth century the Icelanders

143

begin to cultivate a verse form called *rímur*.[5] In form *rímur* comprise a sort of combination of the ancient skaldic poetry and popular medieval European verse. The four-line stanza acquires the more modern end-rime, while at the same time retaining alliteration and kennings. The *rímur* can expand into poems containing hundreds of stanzas, divided into groups or cantos more or less complete in themselves, corresponding to chapters in prose. The subject matter is taken from native or foreign prose narratives, not least of all from the *fornaldarsögur*, and is usually treated with great fidelity in regard to content. Aside from the verse form, the chief innovation in the *rímur* is their more subjective tone. Even though they are narrative poems, the individual *rímur* have introductions consisting of several lyric verses, often of an erotic nature (*mansöngr,* "love poem"). This strong trend toward lyric poetry is prevalent also in other forms of Icelandic literature and is, moreover, a general European phenomenon, of which the Scandinavian ballads are another manifestation. Although the *rímur,* as a whole, are a rather barren form of poetry, they soon came to be prized very highly among the common people. And since they have been chanted to ancient melodies even down to our own time, they have helped to keep the literary tradition alive in Iceland during the dismal centuries following her loss of independence.

Probably no special explanation is needed for the fact that the writing of sagas of native heroes died out. In works such as *Eigla, Laxdœla,* and *Njála* the resources of both substance and style had been exploited to the uttermost degree; to attempt to surpass them was quite out of the question. But even though literary activity sought other means of expression, the question still arises, why artistic quality in the *fornaldarsögur* and *rímur* had to sink so incredibly low. An explanation for this has been sought in the general cultural decline of Iceland. In 1262 the country lost its independence when it came under the rule of the Norwegian crown. During the fourteenth century it was severely and repeatedly plagued by volcanic eruptions, livestock epidemics, and years of famine. Trade and commerce increasingly came under the control of foreigners. Iceland seems to have sunk down into a state of poverty which depressed and blighted all phases of national life.

Good economic conditions do not guarantee the creation of great poetry. On the other hand, one can scarcely imagine that a literature such as the Icelandic sagas of native heroes could be produced in the absence of certain economic conditions. *Njála* could not possibly have been written in a country whose people were on the brink of starvation. The author of this work must have been steeped in an excellent literary culture, and he himself must have had the time and the means to cultivate intellectual interests. In spite of their seemingly popular style, the Sagas of Icelanders are an aristocratic art form, in comparison with which the *fornaldarsögur* and *rímur* impress us as being a very plebeian kind of entertainment, not unlike the serial stories in our modern weekly and monthly magazines. Regardless of how much authentic "history" one can find in the Sagas of Icelanders, they reveal in their portrayal of human beings and in their attitude toward life a genuine and uncompromising sense of realism. They appear to have been created among men of experience, vision, and authority, men who determined their own affairs and those of others. The *rímur*, however, are inferior to the realistic, heroic Sagas of Icelanders in every respect. They seem to have served as a kind of asylum in which one could seek refuge, as a fantasy world in which one could forget the poverty and emptiness of reality and the national isolation and humiliation which followed the fall of the Commonwealth. The feeling of impotence, the consciousness of no longer being able to cope with the problems of life, destroyed the appreciation and the acceptance of reality which are revealed in the great sagas.

At about the time the Icelanders lost their national independence, a significant change occurred within the Icelandic national church. As has already been described, the church in Iceland from the very outset was largely under the control of the secular leaders. Consequently the kind of breach between civil and secular authority and between clergy and laity which existed elsewhere could not develop here. This situation has been regarded as one of the chief prerequisites which made it possible for the sagas to preserve so faithfully the pagan mentality of the Saga Age. But toward the end of the thirteenth century, thanks largely to the efforts of the powerful bishop Árni Þorláksson (d. 1298), the juridical and economic strength of the church was greatly increased. King and church had conquered. The old Icelandic Commonwealth, rooted in a defiant individualism and a pagan view of life, existed no more, either as a political or as a spiritual reality. The fruitful cultural atmosphere, the unique tension betwen old and new ideals to which *Sturlunga* so clearly bears witness, was finally and irretrievably a thing of the past.

CHAPTER 12

The Sagas and Posterity

DURING THE SEVENTEENTH CENTURY a lively interest in the Old Icelandic manuscripts arose among the scholars of Scandinavia. The collection of manuscripts which now began was carried on so vigorously that Iceland soon was scraped almost completely bare of its unique national cultural treasures. Most of these manuscripts landed in Copenhagen. Thus, for example, the Icelandic bishop at Skálholt, Brynjólfr Sveinnsson (1605–1675), in the year 1662 sent the chief manuscript of the *Poetic Edda*, the so-called *codex regius*, as a gift to King Fredrik the Third of Denmark. The foremost collector was the Icelander Árni Magnússon (1663–1730), an official and professor in Copenhagen.[1] With never flagging zeal, perception, and critical judgment he brought together an extraordinarily valuable collection which he bequeathed to the University of Copenhagen. The present curator of the Arnamagnaean Collection is his fellow countryman Jón Helgason (b. 1899), who assumed that office in 1927.[2]

After Iceland in 1944 dissolved its union with Denmark and became a Republic with its own head of state, a request was made on the part of Iceland that the major part of these manuscripts in the Royal Library and the Arnamagnaean Collection be returned. In addition to a "moral" right to these national documents, written by Icelanders in Iceland, arguments of a more objective political nature were adduced in support of this request. The active cooperation of prominent Icelanders in the export of Icelandic manuscripts to Denmark was occasioned solely by the circumstances which prevailed at that time. Iceland was so impoverished that it was not in a position to take care of its easily damaged literary treasures, which were in danger of

moldering away in wretched huts. For responsible Icelanders it was simply a matter of course to try to save them
by sending them to Copenhagen: after all, the university in
that city was also their own cultural center, and Denmark's
king was Iceland's king as well. In recent times, however,
conditions have changed completely. Since 1911 Reykjavík
has had its own university, at which research and editing,
especially in the field of the sagas, are being carried on with
great vigor. As a point of junction for transoceanic air
traffic Iceland has become relatively easily accessible for
foreign scholars on both sides of the Atlantic. The new
Republic, as the heir of the ancient Commonwealth, believes that the time has come to return to their original
home the old Icelandic manuscripts, the proud cultural
heritage which in the eyes of many Icelanders is a symbol
of tiny Iceland's intrinsic worth, of its right to an honorable
place in the circle of independent nations.[3]

The Swedes early took an active part in the collecting
and editing of Icelandic manuscripts. The first printed edition of an Icelandic saga, *Gothrici et Rolfii historia* (*Gaut-
reks saga*), was published by the antiquarian Olof Verelius
(1618–1682) in 1644. This was soon followed by editions of
other sagas including *Bósa saga* (1666), *Hervarar saga* (1672),
and *Sturlaugs saga* (1694).[4] Swedish interest in this literature had a national aspect: scholars during the era of Sweden's political ascendancy sought to find in such sagas,
which they interpreted uncritically as history, confirmation
of Scandinavia's and Sweden's glorious past. Characteristically enough, they concentrated for this purpose on the
more fantastic sagas; all of the sagas mentioned above belong to that category.

But even at this early date Icelandic literature began to
be regarded and studied as an artistic model. In the endeavor of that time to create a Swedish novel, it represented a pattern of no little significance. And, as is well

known, it has continued even down to the present day to be an important stimulus for Scandinavian literature, in choice of subject matter as well as in style. An exhaustive account of this extraordinary influence remains to be written. Of the many writers who with a greater or lesser degree of success have accepted the challenge of the Icelandic sagas it will suffice to mention only a few, all of them well known: Adam Oehlenschläger, Esaias Tegnér, August Strindberg, A. U. Bååth, Selma Lagerlöf, Henrik Ibsen, Björnstjerne Björnson, Sigrid Undset.[5]

It is understandable that the Icelandic sagas should have constituted a much stronger stimulus for the later writers of Iceland itself than for the writers of the other Scandinavian countries. As a model of style the sagas must have had a much deeper significance among Icelanders than anywhere else. This is due in part to the fact that the Icelandic language itself to such an extraordinary degree has preserved the connection with the past. Unlike other Scandinavians, the Icelanders do not have a feeling of moving about in a linguistically strange world when they read their medieval literature in its original form; an Icelandic child who has learned to read has little difficulty in reading for himself the stories of Gunnarr of Hlíðarendi and other heroes. The classic saga style is felt to be an ever living and still timely force in the national cultural tradition.

Among the many Icelandic works of literature which have employed the style and matter of the sagas, Halldór Laxness' *Gerpla* (1952) occupies a prominent position.[6] In a singularly ambitious and consistent manner the author has entered into the ancient tradition; purely as a stylistic exhibition this novel is an ingenious performance. But in spite of everything Laxness, of course, did not write his Icelandic saga from the same point of view as his medieval colleagues. If he had done so, his novel would be merely an imitation, a warming-up of traditional material but no new saga in the sense of an original work with its own problems.

With his uniquely personal saga style the author was able to achieve new effects, not infrequently of an ironic nature. His own day and age also show through in manifold ways, although one must look into his work quite thoroughly in order to notice that.

As a young iconoclast Laxness with devastating arrogance had belittled the national stylistic tradition and had sneered at Snorri and the other "old Icelandic fellows" who endeavored "to collect all sorts of deadly monotonous facts which were of concern to no one" and from whom he, at any rate, had nothing to learn.[7] With his massive saga *Gerpla* the author in the fullness of time has subjected himself to the strict discipline of classical Icelandic prose and of the "old fellows." This is the best evidence of the vital force and continuity of Icelandic culture, of its hold on those who have grown up within its domain. Now Laxness has come to the realization that "an Icelandic author cannot live without constantly having the old books in his thoughts."[8]

APPENDIX

A leaf from one of the oldest and best manuscripts of *Njála*. The manuscript, which is called *Reykjabók* ("Book of Reykir") after the home of its first known owner, Ingjaldur Illugason from Reykir in Miðfjörður, belongs to the famous Arnamagnaean Collection in Copenhagen (see p. 147 above), where it has the signature AM 468 4to. It is dated from about 1300.

Appendix

1. A portion of the facing page (lines 3–12) in literal (diplomatic) transcription. The numerous abbreviations, which have been expanded in the usual manner, are indicated by italics:

G. letr flytia *voro* þei*ra* br*ǫð*ra *til* skips ok þa *er* oll favng .G. *voro* kom*in* *ok* skip *var* miok bvit. þa riðr .G. *til* bergþorshvals *ok* aðra bęi at fina m*enn* *ok* þackaði liðveizlv ollv*m* þ*eim* *er* honv*m* hofðv lið veit*t*. an*n*an dag eptir byr h*ann* fe*rð* sina *til* skips. *ok* sagði þa ollv liði at h*ann* mv*n*di riða í br*ott* alf*ar*i. *ok* þotti monnv*m* þ*at* mikit. en ventv þo t*il*qvamv h*ans* siðaR .G. hverfr *til* allra m*ann*a *er* h*ann* *var* bvin*n* gengv m*enn* vt m*eð* honv*m* all*ir*. h*ann* stingr niðr atg*eir*i*n*um *ok* stiklar i soðvlin*n* *ok* riða þe*i*r kolskeggr í br*ott*. þe*i*r riða fra*m* at markarflioti. þa drap hestr .G. fęti *ok* stok h*ann* af baki. honv*m* varð litið vp*p* *til* hliðarinnar ok bearins at hliða*r*enda ok męlti fog*r* *er* hliðin s*va* at m*er* hef*i*r hon alld*r*i iafn fǫgr synz. blęik*ir* ak*r*ar en slęgín tún *ok* mvn ek riða heím aptr ok *fa*ra hv*er*gi.

2. The same section in normalized Old Icelandic spelling such as is generally used in saga editions and handbooks:

> Gunnarr lætr flytja vǫru þeira brœðra til skips. Ok þá er ǫll fǫng Gunnars váru komin ok skip var mjǫk búit, þá ríðr Gunnarr til Bergþórshváls ok [á] aðra bœi at finna menn ok þakkaði liðveizlu ǫllum þeim, er honum hǫfðu lið veitt.
>
> Annan dag eptir býr hann ferð sína til skips ok sagði þá ǫllu liði, at hann myndi ríða í braut alfari, ok þótti mǫnnum þat mikit, en væntu þó tilkvámu hans síðar. Gunnarr hverfr til allra manna, er hann var búinn. Gengu menn út með honum allir. Hann stingr niðr

atgeirinum ok stiklar í sǫðulinn, ok ríða þeir Kolskeggr
í braut. Þeir ríða fram at Markarfljóti. Þá drap hestr
Gunnars fœti, ok stǫkk hann af baki.

Honum varð litit upp til hlíðarinnar ok bœjarins at
Hlíðarenda ok mælti: "Fǫgr er hlíðin, svá at mér hefir
hon aldri jafnfǫgr sýnzk, bleikir akrar en slegin tún, ok
mun ek ríða heim aptr ok fara hvergi."

3. The same passage in Modern Icelandic. The slight differences between this and the preceding text affect only
the orthography.

Gunnar lætur flytja vöru þeirra bræðra til skips. Og
þá er öll föng Gunnars voru komin og skip var mjög
búið, þá ríður Gunnar til Bergþórshvols og á aðra bæi að
finna menn og þakkaði liðveizlu öllum þeim, er honum
höfðu lið veitt.

Annan dag eftir býr hann ferð sína til skips og sagði
öllu liði, að hann myndi ríða í burt alfarinn, og þótti
mönnum það mikið, en væntu þó tilkomu hans síðar.
Gunnar hverfur til allra manna, er hann var búinn.
Gengu menn út með honum allir. Hann stingur niður
atgeirinum og stiklar í söðulinn, og ríða þeir Kolskeggur
í burt. Þeir ríða fram að Markarfljóti. Þá drap hestur
Gunnars fæti, og stökk hann af baki.

Honum varð litið upp til hlíðarinnar og bæjarins að
Hlíðarenda og mælti: "Fögur er hlíðin, svo að mér hefir
hún aldrei jafnfögur sýnzt, bleikir akrar en slegin tún,
og mun ég ríða heim aftur og fara hvergi."

4. The same passage in Swedish translation:

Gunnarr låter föra sina och sin brors varor ombord
på skeppet. Och när alla förnödenheter hade kommit
och skeppet var nästan segelklart, rider Gunnarr till
Bergþórshváll och även till andra gårdar för att ta farväl
och tackade alla dem, som hade gett honom sitt stöd.
Följande dag gör han sig färdig att rida ned till
skeppet och sade till allt sitt husfolk, att han red bort
för alltid. Detta gick dem alla djupt till sinnes, men de
hoppades likväl, att han en gång skulle komma tillbaka.

När Gunnarr var färdig, tar han avsked av alla, och alla följde honom ut. Han sticker spjutyxan i marken och svingar sig i sadeln. Därpå rida han och Kolskeggr sin väg. De rida fram mot Markarfljót. Då snubblade Gunnars häst, och han kastades ur sadeln. Han kom att se upp mot liden och gården på Hlíðarendi och sade: "Vacker är liden. Aldrig har den tyckts mig så vacker, åkrarna gula och tunen slagna. Jag vill rida hem igen och fara ingenstans."

5. The same passage in English translation:

Gunnarr had his wares and those of his brother brought to the ship. And when this had been done and the ship was about ready to sail, Gunnarr rode to Bergþórshváll and to other farms to say farewell and to thank all those who had given him their support.

On the following day he got ready [early] to ride to the ship, and he told all his people that he was going away for good. They were grieved at this, yet they hoped he would some day return. When he was ready to leave, Gunnarr kissed them all good-by, and they all went out of the house with him. He thrust his halberd into the ground and used it to spring into the saddle. Then he and Kolskeggr rode away.

As they were riding down toward the river Markarfljót, Gunnarr's horse stumbled and he sprang from the saddle. He happened to glance up toward the hillside and the farmstead Hlíðarendi, and he said:

"Fair is the hillside. It has never seemed so fair to me before, with its fallow fields and mown hayfield. I shall ride back home and never leave."

NOTES

Notes

Additions to the author's notes as well as additional notes supplied by the translator are preceded by an asterisk in parentheses.

INTRODUCTION

(*) 1. Despite the wide application of the word *saga* and its frequent occurrence in compounds, the usage of this word seems to cause no confusion among Icelanders. As used by modern scholars of ancient Icelandic literature, *saga* denotes a written prose narrative. (See Preface.)

CHAPTER 1

(*) A well-balanced, detailed history of Iceland until the fall of the Commonwealth (1262) is Jón Jóhannesson, *Íslendinga saga I* ("A History of the Icelanders") (Reykjavík, 1956). Sigurður Nordal's *Íslenzk menning I* ("Icelandic Culture") (Reykjavík, 1942), is a penetrating interpretation of Icelandic culture which is especially important for an understanding of the pagan period. An English translation by Vilhjálmur Bjarnar will be published in the annual *Islandica*. Kristján Eldjárn's detailed and amply illustrated *Kuml og haugfé úr heiðum sið á Íslandi* ("Graves and Antiquities from the Heathen Period in Iceland") (Reykjavík, 1956), sheds welcome light on Icelandic civilization during the Viking Age (*ca.* 875–1000). A useful book in English is Knut Gjerset, *History of Iceland* (New York, 1924).

(*) 1. The question of the date and authorship of *Landnámabók*, which is of fundamental importance for saga research, is critically discussed by Halldór Hermannsson in the introduction to his edition of *Íslendingabók* (1930), and by G. Turville-Petre in *Origins of Icelandic Literature* (Chap. 4). The latter argues convincingly that Ari Þorgilsson began compiling *Landnámabók* as early as the year 1100. The most important monograph on *Landnámabók* is Jón Jóhannesson, *Gerðir Landnámabókar* ("Redactions of *Landnámabók*") (Reykjavík, 1941), which is a meticulous investigation of the texts of the several versions of this document and of their relationship to each other and to some of the sagas.

2. On the *papar* see Einar Ól. Sveinsson, "Papar," *Skírnir*, 119 (1945), 170–203. (*) The same account is given in *Íslendingabók* (Chap. I):

At that time Christian men whom the Norsemen called Papar were here; but afterward they went away because they did not wish to live together with pagans, and they left behind Irish books and bells and staffs. From this it could be seen that they were Irishmen.

(*) 3. The Law Speakers and bishops of Iceland during this period are listed in Jón Jóhannesson's *Íslendinga saga*.

(*) 4. Hereafter the conventional anglicized forms godi (pl., godar), godord, and thingman will be used.

(*) 5. For an illuminating analysis of the composition of this poem and its recitation before the king see Cecil Wood, "The Reluctant Christian and the King of Norway," *Scandinavian Studies*, 31 (1959), 65–72. An excellent discussion of the verse of the "troublesome poet" with translations of several occasional verses will be found in L. M. Hollander, *The Skalds*.

(*) 6. A *hólmganga* was originally a duel fought according to strict rules on a holm, or small island.

(*) 7. The booths mentioned so often in the sagas were temporary abodes at the General Assembly. Their walls were of stone and turf, over which a piece of sailcloth was stretched as a roof during the time they were in use.

(*) 8. This passage from *Kristni saga* (Chap. 12) is similar to the shorter account in *Íslendingabók* (Chap. 7), which evidently was one of its sources. For a more detailed treatment of the subject see Eiríkr Magnússon, "The Conversion of Iceland to Christianity," *The Saga-Book of the Viking Society*, 2 (1901), 348–374.

9. The quotation referred to can be found in Laxness' *Sjálfsagðir hlutir* ("Self-evident Matters") (Reykjavík, 1946), p. 28.

CHAPTER 2

1. This theory has been developed by Barði Guðmundsson, Keeper of the National Archives in Iceland, in a series of papers written in Icelandic and published in the journal *Andvari*. It has been rejected by E. Ó. Sveinsson in the introduction to his edition of *Njáls saga*. (*) See also Sveinsson's *Dating the Icelandic Sagas* (Chap. 9). Barði Guðmundsson's studies on *Njáls saga* are included in a collection of his papers entitled *Höfundur Njálu* ("The Author of *Njála*"), published posthumously (Reykjavík, 1958).

(*) 2. Three excellent papers touching on this problem are E. Ó. Sveinsson, "The Icelandic Sagas and the Period in Which Their Authors Lived," *Acta Philologica Scandinavica*, 12 (1937), 71–90; G. Turville-Petre, "Notes on the Intellectual History of the Icelanders," *History*, 27 (1942), 111–123; and R. George Thomas, "The Sturlung Age as an Age of Saga Writing," *Germanic Review*, 25 (1950), 50–66.

(*) 3. *Sturlunga saga* is available in a complete Danish translation by Kr. Kålund (1904) and in an abridged German one by W. Baetke (1930). For editions see the Translator's Introduction.

4. The Icelandic word *fróðr* means "learned." (*) Since *fróðr* refers chiefly to knowledge of history, it was used as an appellative with the names of the early Icelandic historians (*ca.* 1050–1150) and a few later ones. The venerable Bede was also thus honored.

CHAPTER 3

In connection with this chapter the reader is referred to E. Ó. Sveinsson, *Sturlungaöld* (Reykjavík, 1940). This sensitive and perspicuous study is available in an English translation by Jóhann S. Hannesson, *The Age of the Sturlungs: Icelandic Civilization in the Thirteenth Century* (1953). (*) Further literature on the period is listed by Sveinsson and by Hannesson in the author's and translator's prefaces. (See also note 2 to Chap. 2 above.)

(*) 1. The word *þáttr* (pl., *þættir*), which literally means "strand of a rope," is used metaphorically to designate either a section of a longer story or an independent short tale. A translation of *Stúfs þáttr* is found in H. G. Leach's anthology *A Pageant of Old Scandinavia*.

2. The quotations are from *Byskupa sögur* (Reykjavík, 1948), 1, 137, 150–151.

3. E. Ó. Sveinsson, *Sturlungaöld*, p. 75.

4. The slaying of Sighvatr and Sturla is related in *Sturlunga saga*, 2, 143.

CHAPTER 4

(*) The most detailed treatment of the beginnings of vernacular prose writing in Iceland is found in G. Turville-Petre's *Origins of Icelandic Literature*. For briefer discussions see Stefán Einarsson, *A History of Icelandic Literature*, and Sigurður Nordal, *Sagalitteraturen*. The Christian poetry of the period is treated thoroughly by Wolfgang Lange in his *Studien zur Christlichen Dichtung der Nordgermanen* (1958).

(*) 1. An exemplary edition of this work is *First Grammatical Treatise: The Earliest Germanic Phonology*. An edition, translation, and commentary by Einar Haugen (1950).

(*) 2. On this point cf. the statement of Turville-Petre, *op. cit.,* p. 142: "In a word, the learned literature did not teach the Icelanders what to think or what to say, but it taught them how to say it. It is unlikely that the sagas of kings and of Icelanders, or even the sagas of ancient heroes, would have developed as they did unless several generations of Icelanders had first been trained in hagiographic narrative."

(*) 3. This factor is strongly emphasized by Stefán Einarsson in the introduction to his *History of Icelandic Literature,* where he speaks of the "immigrant escape literature" of the Icelanders which, together with their interest in history, he attributes largely to their "uprooting from the old country" and their "nostalgic memories" of the homeland.

(*) 4. On *Landnámabók* see note 1 to Chap. 1.

(*) 5. The importance of Sæmundr and his descendants is discussed by Halldór Hermannsson in *Sæmund Sigfússon and the Oddaverjar* (1932).

(*) 6. *Íslendingabók* has been edited with English translation, critical introduction, and copious annotation by Halldór Hermannsson (1930).

7. The standard work on Snorri is Sigurður Nordal, *Snorri Sturluson* (Reykjavík, 1920). A detailed study in Swedish is Gustav Cederschiöld, *Snorre Sturluson och hans verk* (Stockholm, 1922).

(*) 8. The standard edition is that of Bjarni Aðalbjarnarson: *Snorri Sturluson, Heimskringla* (Reykjavík, 1941–1951). *Ynglinga saga* has been edited separately by Elias Wessén in the *Nordisk filologi* series. For translations and studies, see the Translator's Introduction.

(*) 9. Nordal has summarized the evidence for Snorri's authorship of *Egils saga* in the Introduction to his edition of that work.

(*) 10. The non-specialist can gain at least an inkling of the exceedingly intricate nature of this poetry from Cecil Wood's paper "Concerning the Interpretation of Skaldic Verse," *Germanic Review,* 33 (1958), 293–305, and from Hollander's translations in *The Skalds.*

(*) 11. This portion of Snorri's *Edda* is available in English translations by A. G. Brodeur and Jean I. Young. For a concise discussion of this work see Anne Holtsmark, "Edda," *Kulturhistorisk leksikon III,* cols. 475–480, where the most important critical literature is cited.

(*) 12. The *Poetic Edda* has been translated into English by H. A. Bellows and by Lee M. Hollander. Anne Holtsmark has discussed the most important problems of research on this work in her paper "Eddadiktning," *Kulturhistorisk leksikon III,* cols. 480–488. For a more detailed treatment see Jón Helgason, *Noregs og Islands digtning* in *Nordisk kultur VIII B* (1953), and Stefán Einarsson, *A History of Icelandic Literature.*

(*) 13. See note 1 above.

(*) 14. For an authoritative statement on this genre see E. Ó. Sveinsson, "Fornaldarsögur Norðrlanda," *Kulturhistorisk leksikon II,* cols. 499–507.

15. "Time and Vellum," published in the *Annual Bulletin of the Modern Humanities Research Association,* 24 (1952), 15–26.

CHAPTER 5

1. Björn M. Ólsen stated his views in a paper entitled "Om Gunnlaugs Saga Ormstungu" published in *Det kgl. danske Videnskabernes Selskabs Skrifter,* 7 Række, hist. og fil. Afd. II, 1 (1911). Finnur Jónsson's reply is found in the Introduction to his edition of this saga (1916). (*) Modern scholarship agrees on the whole with Ólsen. For succinct discussions of the problem see the Introduction to the edition by Peter G. Foote (1957), and the English summary of Bjarni Einarsson, *Skáldasögur* (1961).

2. Paul Rubow, "De islandske Sagaer," published in his *Smaa kritiske Breve* (1936), and in an English translation, "The Sagas" in *Two Essays* (1949). (*) While Rubow undoubtedly goes too far in this respect, it is interesting to note that the literary historian James Carney in his book *Studies in Irish Literature and History* (1955) independently comes to conclusions similar to Rubow's regarding the influence of the Tristan *legend* on the sagas. This theory has been developed by Bjarni Einarsson in his study *Skáldasögur* ("Sagas of Skalds").

(*) 3. In English translation: *The Origin of the Icelandic Family Sagas* (1930).

4. The anecdote about the young Icelander and Haraldr harðráði is from the well-known codex *Morkinskinna.* It is found in volume 12 of the *Íslendinga sögur* (1947), p. 175 f.

(*) 5. This feature of style has been investigated by W. Lehmann, *Das Präsens historicum in den Íslendinga sögur* (1939) and by Ulrike Sprenger, *Praesens Historicum und Praeteritum in der Altisländischen Saga* (1951), but their conclusions are unconvincing.

6. In his book *Storhetstid* (1922), p. 4.

(*) 7. Nordal's monograph is now available in an English translation by R. George Thomas (1959). It might be added here that E. V. Gordon had independently arrived at conclusions similar to Nordal's in a paper published in *Medium Ævum,* 8 (1939), 1–32.

(*) 8. Quite recently, however, A. R. Taylor has discovered "A Source for *Hrafnkels Saga*," *Saga-Book,* 15 (1959), 130–137. See also the Introduction to *Austfirðinga sögur,* edited by Jón Jóhannesson (1950). English translations of *Hrafnkels saga* by Gwyn Jones will be found in his *Four Icelandic Sagas* and in his *Eirik the Red.* The most convenient editions for students are those of F. S. Cawley (1932) and W. Baetke (1952), which have glossaries in English and German, respectively. An informative study is Randolph Quirk, "Textual Notes on Hrafnkelssaga," *London Mediaeval Studies,* 2 (1951), 1–31.

9. Two recent papers in English on this problem are Gwyn Jones, "History and Fiction in the Sagas of the Icelanders," *Saga-Book,* 13

(1952-1953), 285–306, and Sigurður Nordal, "The Historical Element in the Icelandic Family Sagas," *The W. P. Ker Memorial Lectures*, Vol. 15 (1957).

10. For a perceptive interpretation of the sagas as works of narrative art see E. Ó. Sveinsson, "The Value of the Icelandic Sagas," *Saga-Book*, 15 (1957–1959), 1–16.

CHAPTER 6

The style of the Sagas of Icelanders has been treated in numerous studies: R. Heinzel, *Beschreibung der isländischen Saga* (1880); A. U. Bååth, *Studier öfver kompositionen i några isländska ättsagor* (1885); A. Goedecke, *Die Darstellung der Gemütsbewegungen in der isländischen Familiensaga* (1933); H. J. Graf, *Untersuchungen zur Gebärde in der Íslendingasaga* (1939); Margaret Jeffrey, *The Discourse in Seven Icelandic Sagas* (1934); W. Ludwig, *Untersuchungen über den Entwicklungsgang und die Funktion des Dialogs in der isländischen Saga* (1934). Fine observations on style and character delineation are found in W. P. Ker's essay mentioned in the Translator's Introduction as well as in many investigations of individual sagas such as Nordal's monograph on *Hrafnkels saga* and Sveinsson's books on *Njála*.

(*) The best introduction in English to this many-faceted problem is O. Springer, "The Style of the Icelandic Family Sagas," *Journal of English and Germanic Philology*, 38 (1939), 107–128, which provides a comprehensive survey of the field, a critical discussion of previous studies with thorough documentation, and concrete suggestions for future studies.

1. *Germanentum* (1934), p. 136 f.

(*) 2. Occasionally, however, we find saga writers using synonyms, apparently for the purpose of avoiding monotony. In *Eyrbyggja saga*, for example, a battle is referred to on the same page by the words *bardagi*, *skipti*, and *fundr* (Chap. 18). Similarly, in the same saga a bed is called *rekkja*, *rúm*, and *sæng*; and *bera inn heyit* alternates with *leggja inn heyit* (Chap. 37), *rísa upp* with *standa upp* (Chap. 36), and *öndvegi* with *hásæti* (Chap. 33). Furthermore, there seems to have been a conscious avoidance of hackneyed similes and alliterative phrases, such as we frequently find in the *riddarasögur*, *fornaldarsögur*, and some of the *byskupasögur*. On this point see P. Schach, "The Use of the Simile in the Old Icelandic Family Sagas," *Scandinavian Studies*, 24 (1952), 149–165.

(*) 3. A case in point is the fact that the history of modern Icelandic literature (1800–1940) has recently been treated in two separate volumes by two different scholars: Stefán Einarsson, *History of Icelandic*

Prose Writers (1948) and Richard Beck, *History of Icelandic Poets* (1950).

(*) 4. For a brief study of one of the most characteristic uses of natural scenery see P. Schach, "The Anticipatory Literary Setting in the Old Icelandic Sagas," *Scandinavian Studies*, 27 (1955), 1–13.

(*) 5. This famous passage has elicited much scholarly controversy and inspired various intrepretations. Guðmundur Finnbogason, "Náttúrufeguró í fornbókmenntum vorum," *Skírnir*, 117 (1943), 180–187, emphasizes Gunnarr's appreciation of the natural beauty of his home district. Rolf Pipping, "Et dubbeltydigt omen," *Budkavlen*, 15 (1936), 80–82, explains Gunnarr's decision on the basis of a folk belief about falling to the ground. And Otto Springer uses Gunnarr's leap into the saddle without using the stirrups as the starting point for an interesting study of "The 'âne stegreif' Motif in Medieval Literature," *Germanic Review*, 11 (1950), 391–403. Most of the studies center upon the problem of Gunnarr's motive or motives for defying the verdict of the General Assembly and the question of whether his attitude toward nature was a farmerly or a purely esthetic one.

(*) 6. On this point see Lee M. Hollander, "Verbal Periphrasis and Litotes in Old Norse," *Monatshefte*, 30 (1938), 182–189, and "Litotes in Old Norse," *PMLA*, 53 (1938), 1–33. The excellent monograph by Maria Müller on the *Verhüllende Metaphorik in der Saga* (1939) affords new insights into the psychological significance of the subdued, restrained language of the sagas.

(*) 7. Verses 76 and 77 from *Hávamál* are so important for an understanding of the saga characters and their life values and ideals (discussed in Chap. 8) that they will be quoted here:

> Deyr fé,   deyja frændr,
> deyr sjálfr it sama;
> en orztírr   deyr aldregi
> þeim er sér góðan getr.

> Deyr fé,   deyja frændr,
> deyr sjálfr it sama;
> ek veit einn   at aldri deyr:
> dómr um dauðan hvern.

[Cattle die, kinsmen die, and so each one will die; but fame never dies for him who has well earned it.
Cattle die, kinsmen die, and so each one will die; I know one thing that never dies: the repute of every dead man.]

(*) 8. And this description also underscores indirectly an important trait of Egill's character: avarice. As soon as the king gives Egill a precious golden ring from his arm, Egill's grief-tortured features relax and he begins to drink and converse with the other guests. King Ethelstan also gives Egill two chests of silver which he is to share with his father Skalla-Grímr; but Egill can never quite bring himself to give his aged father his share of the money in spite of Skalla-Grímr's discreet hints that he would like to have it!

(*) 9. Snorri goði is similarly described in *Eyrbyggja saga* (Chap. 15) at that point of the story at which he assumes the dominant role. This aspect of saga style and construction has been imitated in some of the *lygisögur*, notably the *Saga af Tristram ok Ysodd*.

10. On this point see Sveinn Bergsveinsson, "Sagaen og den haardkogte Roman," *Edda,* 42 (1942), 56–62. (*) A recent paper in English is Julia McGrew's "Faulkner and the Icelanders," *Scandinavian Studies,* 31 (1959), 1–14. Miss McGrew stresses less the similarity of external technique than the similarity of themes and intent.

CHAPTER 7

In connection with this chapter see Margaret Haeckel, *Die Darstellung und Funktion des Traumes in der isländischen Familiensaga* (1934), and Georgia Dunham Kelchner, *Dreams in Old Norse Literature and Their Affinities in Folklore* (1935). (*) The former emphasizes the psychological, esthetic, and stylistic functions of the prophetic dream; the latter lists all the texts with English translation. G. Turville-Petre, "Dreams in Icelandic Tradition," *Folklore,* 69 (1958), 93–111, is a stimulating and penetrating analysis of the problem.

(*) 1. Although "presumptuous and optimistic" Þorkell's interpretation of this dream is not too surprising when we consider that it is very similar to several variants of the well-known tree dream. On this type of prophetic dream see the study of Turville-Petre mentioned above (esp. pp. 93–96) and P. Schach, "Some Parallels to the Tree Dream in *Ruodlieb*," *Monatshefte,* 46 (1954), 353–364.

(*) 2. Various interpretations of this dualism and the meaning of the dream women have been advanced. The problem is touched upon in several recent studies on this saga in English: G. Turville-Petre, "Gísli Súrsson and His Poetry: Traditions and Influences," *Modern Language Review,* 39 (1944), 374–391; Ida L. Gordon, "The Origins of Gíslasaga," *Saga-Book,* 13 (1949–1950), 183–205; Anne Holtsmark, *Studies in the Gísla saga* (1951); and Taylor Culbert, "The Construction of the Gísla saga," *Scandinavian Studies,* 31 (1959), 151–165. The most convenient edition is that of Agnete Loth (1956); the somewhat abridged German translation of F. Ranke (1938) is readable, as is also the English one by Ralph B. Allen (1936), despite its occasional archaisms and numerous inaccuracies.

3. On this point see Bååth's detailed and thorough analysis of the structure of the sagas mentioned in the introductory note to Chap. 6. The fatalism of the sagas is treated by W. Wirth, *Der Schicksalsglaube in den Isländersagas: Eine religionsgeschichtlich-philologische Untersuchung über Wesen und Bedeutung der altgermanischen Vorstellungen von Schicksal und Glück* (1940).

CHAPTER 8

In connection with this chapter the reader is referred to W. Gehl, *Ruhm und Ehre bei den Nordgermanen: Studien zum Lebensgefühl der isländischen Saga* (1937). (*) Another study dealing with the problem is Matthías Jónasson, "Die Grundnormen des Handelns bei den Isländern heidnischer Zeit," *Beiträge zur Geschichte der deutschen Sprache und Literatur*, 67 (1945–1946), 139–184.

(*) 1. Hel, the goddess of the underworld, was thought of as being half black and half flesh-colored. The agitation of Flosi is underscored by the use of three similes—the only occurrence of such a piling up of similes in the Sagas of Icelanders.

(*) 2. "Dry food" included, in addition to herbs, fruits, nuts, grains, and vegetables, the flesh of fish and whales, but not that of seals and walruses. See note 1 to p. 138 in E. Ó. Sveinsson's edition of *Laxdœla saga* (1934).

(*) 3. The verse, of which the first half is here quoted, is found in Vol. 2, Chap. 49 of *Sturlunga saga*.

CHAPTER 9

(*) 1. An English translation by Margaret Schlauch is found in *Three Icelandic Sagas* (1950).

(*) 2. This episode is referred to in Chap. 7.

CHAPTER 10

(*) 1. For an English translation which preserves the alliterative form of the original see L. M. Hollander, *The Skalds*.

(*) 2. Rán was the goddess of the sea; according to Snorri's *Skáldskaparmál* (Chap. 33), she had a net with which she sought to catch all men who went to sea. Rán's husband was the sea-god Ægir.

(*) 3. Egill had two daughters and two other sons in addition to his favorite son Böðvarr. Gunnarr had died shortly before the drowning of Böðvarr; Þorsteinn, who was quite unlike his father, inherited the farm at Borg. One of his daughters was Helga in fagra, heroine of *Gunnlaugs saga*.

(*) 4. Óðinn, supreme deity in the Norse pantheon, had many functions and many names; he was not only the god of victory and of the dead, but also of wisdom and poetry. It was in the latter capacity that Egill had to pay homage to him, albeit reluctantly.

(*) 5. On the goddess Hel see note 1 to Chap. 8.

(*) 6. In a most stimulating study, "Jorvikferden: Et vendepunkt i Egil Skallagrimssons liv," *Edda*, 46 (1947), 145–248, Hallvard Lie has argued brilliantly but unconvincingly that the author of *Egils saga* did not fully understand the complex personality of the historical Egill.

7. Nordal's views on Snorri as the author of *Egils saga* are concisely stated in the introduction to his edition of that saga (1933).

(*) 8. For a stimulating study of the "sagas of poets" see Bjarni Einarsson, *Skáldasögur* (1961).

9. In his study *Á Njálsbúð: Bók um mikið listaverk* (*In Njall's Booth: A Book about a Great Work of Art*) (Reykjavík, 1943), E. Ó. Sveinsson has given the most penetrating analysis we have of the portrayal of character and the view of life as presented in an individual saga. (*) A concise summary of Sveinsson's perceptive interpretation of this work in Swedish is contained in his paper "Njáls saga," *Scripta Islandica*, 1 (1950), 3–43.

(*) 10. Recently, however, I. R. Maxwell has eloquently defended the apparently episodic nature of this portion of the saga in his perceptive study, "Pattern in *Njáls Saga*," *Saga-Book*, 15 (1957–1959), 17–47.

(*) 11. Especially noteworthy are the Fróðá marvels (Chap. 50–55), following the arrival there and the death of the Hebridean woman Þorgunna.

CHAPTER 11

(*) 1. The most detailed study to date of this genre is Margaret Schlauch, *Romance in Iceland* (1934). The introduction to Åke Lagerholm's exemplary edition of *Drei Lygisǫgur* (1927) in the *Altnordische Saga-Bibliothek* is also very informative.

(*) 2. On this saga see H. G. Leach, *Angevin Britain and Scandinavia* (Chap. 7); and P. Schach, "Some Observations on *Tristrams Saga*," *Saga-Book*, 15 (1957–1959), 102–129, and "The *Saga af Tristram ok Ísodd*: Summary or Satire?" *Modern Language Quarterly*, 21 (1960), 336–352.

(*) 3. *Örvar-Odds saga* has been edited by R. C. Boer (1892) in the *Altnordische Saga-Bibliothek*.

(*) 4. A good edition of *Friðþjófs saga* is that of Ludvig Larsson (1901) in the *Altnordische Saga-Bibliothek*. An English translation of Tegnér's poetic adaptation by W. L. Blackley is found in *Poems by Tegnér* (1914).

(*) 5. For a more detailed account of the *rímur* see the English introduction to Sir William Craigie's three-volume anthology *Sýnisbók islenzkra rímna* ("Specimens of Icelandic Rímur") (London, 1952).

CHAPTER 12

(*) 1. Árni Magnússon was secretary in the Danish Royal Archives until 1701, when he became the first professor of Danish antiquities in the University of Copenhagen.

(*) 2. For a concise statement of Jón Helgason's significance as poet, scholar, and editor see Stefán Einarsson, *A History of Icelandic Literature*, pp. 313–314 and *passim*.

(*) 3. The controversy arising from the Icelanders' request that this precious cultural heritage be returned has been widely discussed in European, especially Danish and Icelandic, newspapers. The Icelandic case is cogently stated by E. Ó. Sveinsson in his booklet *Handritamálið* ("The Matter of the Manuscripts") (Reykjavík, 1959). This has been ably and sympathetically reviewed by L. M. Hollander in *Scandinavian Studies*, 33 (1961), 249–250.

4. For a recent study on this topic see Gun Nilsson, "Den isländska litteraturen i stormaktstidens Sverige," *Scripta Islandica*, 5 (1954), 19–41.

5. The most comprehensive and thorough work on the influence of the Icelandic sagas on the style tradition in later Scandinavian prose is P. V. Rubow, *Saga og Pastiche: Bidrag til dansk Prosahistorie* (1923).

(*) 6. This novel has been translated by Katherine John under the title *The Happy Warriors* (1958).

7. In a letter by Laxness dated April 17, 1923.

8. In the essay collection *Sjálfsagðir hlutir* (Reykjavík, 1946), p. 9.

(*) It is significant in this connection that Laxness has recently edited a book *Islandsk saga* (1958) containing three essays on the sagas, one of them by the Nobel prize winner himself.

INDEX

Index

THE AUTHOR

Docent Peter Hallberg has contributed significantly to Icelandic-Swedish literary understanding through his numerous articles in Icelandic and Swedish journals and through his translations and interpretations of the works of Laxness in Sweden. Among his publications in this field are *Halldór Kiljan Laxness* (1952) and *Den store vävaren: En studie i Laxness' ungdomsdiktning* ("The Great Weaver: A Study in the Early Writings of Laxness") (1954). Since 1951 he has been a docent in literary history at the University of Göteborg.

THE TRANSLATOR

Before coming to the University of Nebraska in 1951, Professor Paul Schach was Head of the German Department at North Central College. He has also taught at Albright College, and has been a visiting lecturer at the University of Pennsylvania and the University of Colorado. His articles, book reviews, and translations have appeared in the *Journal of English and Germanic Philology*, *Scandinavian Studies*, *Modern Language Quarterly*, *American Speech*, and many other scholarly periodicals on both sides of the Atlantic. His translation of *Eyrbyggja Saga* (with Lee M. Hollander), published by the University of Nebraska Press in 1959, "will take its place among the landmarks of translation" (Hedin Brunner, *Scandinavian Studies*).